Daily Assignment
Effective Teaching Strategies

By Linda Fobes

To my most favorite student, teacher, and friend. You are an inspiration.

Best Effort
&
Much love,
Linda

1

Dedicated to teachers everywhere...

...with admiration for all they do.

TABLE OF CONTENTS

Chapter 3: Classroom Management Strategies 47
Daily Assignment:

Chapter 4: Basic Background Knowledge   69
Daily Assignment:

Chapter 5: Scaffolding Learning for Students 100
Daily Assignment:

Chapter 6: Effective Strategies For Teachers 132
Daily Assignment:

Chapter 7: Effective Learning Strategies To Teach Students 147
Daily Assignment:

Chapter 8: Messages Teachers Send and Receive

Chapter 9: End of the Year   168

Chapter 10: Final thoughts   177

CHAPTER 1: GETTING STARTED

Schools Open

Daily Assignment #1: Where to begin?

Well, it's that time of year. Where to begin? What do I need to begin? How do I set up my classroom? Where should I put the teacher's and students' desk? How do I create a learning environment? How do I greet the students and parents on the first day? How should I handle a child crying on the first day? How do I get the parents out of the classroom on the first day so I can begin? What do I say at a parent conference? So many questions…. HELP!!!

I would like to help you. I would like to share, with you, my 34 years of teaching experience. I have taught grades 1, 2, 3, 5, and 6. I have also been an educational consultant for 18 years. I taught a graduate course on effective teaching strategies to K-12 teachers. I retired in June 2010 and would now like to share my knowledge and skills with you.

Robert Marzano, a leading researcher in education, has identified a "Top 9" list of effective teaching strategies, which contribute to higher levels of student achievement:

1. *Identifying similarities and differences*
2. *Summarizing and note taking*
3. *Reinforcing effort and providing recognition*

4. *Homework and practice*
5. *Nonlinguistic representations such as mental images, graphs, acting out content*
6. *Cooperative learning*
7. *Setting objectives and providing feedback*
8. *Generating and testing hypotheses*
9. *Activating prior knowledge via questions, cues, advance   organizers*

Source: Marzano, 2003

I will cover these topics and many more in this book. All of the strategies included in this book are research- based, meaning they will make a difference in student learning.

So, having said all that, let's begin. The first thing you need to do is to get a class list with the students' addresses, parent contact information and birthdates (to be used later). Write a welcome letter to your students. Let the students know how excited you are about the school year and being their teacher. Include something that they should look for on the first day when they come in, e.g. something special/new in the classroom. Also, include a letter to the parents describing a typical school day (schedule), supplies their child will need for the first day, your contact info, a routine, e.g. snacks, birthday celebrations, drop off and pickup procedures and how much you are looking forward to working with them to support their child's learning.

I hope you will experiment with all the strategies included in this book. My goal is to help you build your repertoire.

Please know it took me 35 years to learn all these strategies. If you experiment with one or two every few months you are doing really well.

Daily Assignment #2: Creating a Classroom Environment

At this point, the setup of the classroom needs to be designed. You need to think about the needs of your incoming students and how you plan to teach. Do you want a teacher-centered environment or a student- centered environment? Should there be learning centers, table groupings, or horseshoe arrangement of desk? Where should the teacher's desk be placed? Should there be a place to have community meetings? How will students move about the room? There is a lot to think about. For me, an important piece was to make sure that no matter where I was standing in the room I could see everyone.

In regard to the teacher's desk, I did not have one. I hooked a shoe bag over a closet door for my supplies and used a counter, or something similar to a bookcase, for my desktop. Not having a large teacher's desk provided more space and flexibility in my classroom arrangement. I liked having an arrangement with flexibility. I could move furniture easily for plays, movies, class breakfasts, presentations, etc. I also used large tables instead of desks for my students. However, I did have a few desks if students wanted a separate space. The students had storage bins for their supplies. They also had these great "seat jackets" with pockets to hold immediate materials and supplies. They kept pencils, erasers, scissors, folders, etc... in the pockets. These seat jackets eliminated the need for the students to get up and find the materials and roam the room, which usually led to some other behaviors, such as never coming back.

The design of the classroom is an integral part of classroom management. Students must be able to see the teacher and any visuals that are being used. No student should have his or her back to a teacher.

The design of the classroom also sends a message to the students as to what is important to the teacher. Does the teacher want students to work independently or collaboratively? Is community important? This brings me right back to---- do you want a teacher centered or a child-centered environment?

Daily Assignment #3: Out of Pocket Expenses

This is a hot topic for teachers. How much should you spend from out of pocket expenses be for art supplies, general materials, books, anything that will make your life easier? A ballpark figure is $400-$500 a year, if you're lucky. Every year, for 35 years, I would spend about that amount. Some of my colleagues would spend even more.

Some school districts will reimburse teachers, up to a certain amount, providing they have receipts. Some schools have a fund set aside for reimbursements to teachers. And then there are some schools that allow individual classrooms to do fundraising to offset classroom expenses. One year I had the students paint an old wooden classroom chair with representations of units of study and then raffled it off.

Bottom line: Be prepared for out-of-pocket expenses for those little things that are not included in your budget and save all your receipts. Check with your school administration and colleagues to find out ways, if any, you can be reimbursed. Furthermore, some states offer income tax deductions for these expenses.

Daily Assignment #4: Plans for the 1st Day

In planning the first day there are several things to keep in mind. First, consider specialist, lunch and other events, which will impact your schedule. Then begin planning around them. Be prepared. Have everything Xerox, collated, cut out, stapled, whatever is needed. You will be much more relaxed with these things done. You will also be ready to focus on the students and parents as they come in.

Beginning with a community building activity on the first day is essential. Having a class meeting brings everyone together and helps to get the parents out of the room. Have the students sit in a circle, say their names, and share something about one special person they had an opportunity to spend time with over the summer. This stem equalizes the conversation. Make sure you share as well.

Post the schedule for the day and read it to them, so that the students know what will be happening and that there will be an end to the school day. I wouldn't put the times next to the activities because those first few days never play out the way you want. Some students will challenge you if you are late or early for the next activity.

After sharing they will need a get up and move activity. They could do a writing activity at their new seats. This can take many forms depending on the grade level. In the lower grades you may need to teach how to write a letter of the alphabet. Start with a straight-line letter, such as I or t. For older students, have them write a story. It might be about what they shared about the special person.

They probably need some type of break by now. You could introduce a routine at this point. It might be how to get in a line. Remember, any routine you introduce needs to be taught. Don't assume they know how to do it. Tell them what they will be doing and the purpose of it. Then model it and let them practice it. Give them feedback and have them practice it again and do it frequently. Take them for a walk around the building. Even though they may have been in this building for several years, it is still a new year, with a new teacher. Never assume!

If you can, now might be a good time to let them go outside to play. You will probably need fresh air yourself.

You should include silent reading, which would be best after a lot of movement activity, such as recess. This would also be an opportunity to listen to the students read. This is a form of informal assessment.

Also, find a moment for you to read to the students, it might be a picture book or a short story that relates to the beginning of school or the first unit of study you will be teaching. Match the story to the grade level.

As students finish, you could have an art activity set up for them to draw a self-portrait. You will need to first explain the activity and have a model of how it should look- full page or half page, details, background. If you do this it eliminates the game of "guess what's on the teacher's mind."

Another activity- I swear by this one for lots of reasons- "scrolls" or as some students mistakenly call them "squirrels." (refer to Daily Assignment # 91: Number Scrolls) Prepare for each child a cardboard paper towel roll. Tape a sheet of 1 " graph paper to it. In each box, on the top row, write the numbers -9 to 0. On the second row, write the numbers 1-6, the students will complete this row and continue on to the next. On the inside of the roll, write the student's name. This is essential. It will save a lot of aggravation when someone can't find their scroll or mixes it up with someone else's. As students finish one page, you add another page. They just keep writing numbers at their own pace. I have students do this all year long. It is a content- related filler as well. The highest number a student got to, within 2 years, was 13,678. Again, this becomes an assessment tool. You quickly find out who can count and write numbers correctly, and who does reversals and transposing of numbers. Also, you will discover who understands place value, can recognize patterns, and likes or doesn't like challenges.

Don't try to do all your assessments on the first day. I found observation was the most informative activity for me the first 2 days. Having the students share in the morning can tell you a lot about their comfort levels and oral communication. The writing activity informs you as to their handwriting ability or their story writing ability. The scrolls are full of assessment information.

Are you exhausted yet? It's probably 1:00. It shouldn't be 9:00! Or we're in trouble.

Now you need an afternoon activity. How about letting them experiment with math manipulatives? They will have fun and you will be observing and noting their behaviors. I would only pull out 2-3 types. Remember to explain how to use them and how to clean up when they are done.

At the end of the day introduce a clean-up routine. State what the routine is and the purpose of it, model it, let them practice it, give feedback, and have them practice it again. You need to be tenacious about any routine you teach that is important to you. More about this later.

Most importantly, over plan! Better to have extra than not enough. Trust me on this one.

Make sure you laugh. This has got to be the funniest job ever.

Now, if you have made it through the day, you are to go home, have a glass of wine, a chocolate dessert, and go to bed early because it all begins again tomorrow.

Best Effort!

Daily Assignment #5: Community Building Activity "Artifact Bags"

I would like to share with you a community building activity. This makes a great 1st homework assignment. The name of this activity is "Artifact Bags" or "About Me Bags." I have used this strategy with first and second graders, as well as with adults.

Each student will need a brown paper lunch bag. They are to place 4 objects inside which represent them. For example, I would put a small book to represent my love for reading, a tiny fake apple for teaching, a piece of chocolate for my love of chocolate, and a small set of knitting needles for, you guessed it, knitting. Have them put a photo of themselves in the bag as well. No names.

Collect all the bags in a large decorated box. Throughout the first 2 weeks of school you will share these bags with the whole class, and they will guess who the person is, based on the contents. If the class guesses correctly you take the photo out. If they don't guess correctly, you put everything back into the bag, and you do that one again another time.

You have to prep the students before you begin because they get very excited when their bag is being shared and give away whose it belongs to. So, you need to talk to them about body language and not calling out what the objects represent.

This is a great strategy for students to discover what they have in common with each other. It helps everyone to learn something they may not know about their friends.

Don't forget to include a bag for yourself.

There are many ways to develop rules for a classroom. Some teachers have a set list of rules. Some teachers follow the guidelines of Responsive Classroom in establishing rules. I chose to work with the students on developing "The Rule." That's right. One rule. I know that is shocking. But it only takes one rule. And it is "RESPECT EACH OTHER!"

I would like to share with you a unit that I designed for establishing "The Rule." This unit has 4 lessons but may take 4-6 days to complete.

Select 3 books, which reflect some form of chaos in an environment. I chose _The Mystery of the Red Mitten,_ by Steven Kellogg; _Noah's Ark_, by Peter Spier and _Old MacDonald Had An Apartment House_, by Judith Barrett.

Divide the class into 3 groups. Depending on the grade level, have the students, or an adult, read one of the stories to a group. Each group should have a large sheet of paper with an outline of the environment depicted in the story they are reading, e.g. red mitten, ark, apartment house.

Before the stories are read, ask the students to think about "What might one rule have been, for the characters in the story, to prevent all the chaos?"

Establish roles within the group, e.g. summarizer of the story, rule presenter(s), recorder(s), timekeeper.

After the groups have read their story, they are to write down all the rules they thought about onto the large paper. Establish a minimum and maximum amount of rules because it can get out of control, or you might end up with nothing). Depending on the age group, someone will need to be the recorder. This part of the lesson may take 20-30 minutes. Setting a timer will help to move the conversation along and keep the groups focused, hence a timekeeper.

While students are waiting for groups to finish, the other groups may draw details on their large paper, e.g. staircase, animals, etc.

When all groups have completed listing their rules, bring the class back together and have each group do a presentation. Begin with story summarizer, then presenter(s) of rules. Process the 3 groups' work and list the common rules, while also pointing out that each environment had different rules as well. Use the word "respect" while processing. Post charts.

This lesson may take 2 days, depending on the age/grade of students.

For homework, have the students list rules for their home. On the following day, process the homework with the students. What are the common rules? Which rules are family- specific? Again, use the word "respect". You might also put them back into their groups and have them come up with the answers to the 2 questions. With the whole group process the activity. Post the homework.

Daily Assignment #7: Lessons 3+4 for Establishing Classroom Rules

For **Lesson 3** you will need a large floor plan of the school playground and cafeteria. As a whole group, have the students design rules for each floor plan (try to combine some), e.g. no throwing food in the cafeteria, only go down the slide, no hitting. With each suggestion have a quick discussion, "If this was done would it be respectful or disrespectful? What would disrespectful/respectful behavior look like?" An example might be: Rule: Only go down the slide. "Is that being disrespectful or respectful?" "Respectful." "Who are you respecting?" "Friends." "What would disrespectful behavior look like?" "Going up the slide." "Who are you disrespecting?" "Friends."

Point out that different behaviors are necessary for different spaces. But there is one behavior that seems to be very important. "What is that behavior?" As Aretha Franklin would say, R-E-S-P-E-C-T!

Lesson 4 pulls it all together. You will need a large floor plan of the classroom.

As a whole group, have the students design rules for the class. Process with the group and see if any of them can be combined. Have the same discussion for each rule, as you did in Lesson 3.

Hopefully, they will recognize the importance of always being respectful and that it is the key to all appropriate behavior. Students may want to keep all the rules up. Make sure the word RESPECT is on the chart in large letters.

Post all the charts so that the students can see their progression through this process.

Remember, you are the model of the behaviors you want your students to demonstrate (so, don't go up the slide). And, they are watching. They are watching to see how you speak to colleagues, as well as to them. Also, remember to watch your body language. More on body language later.

This unit, and the books that go with it, can be used at almost every grade level. The older students will enjoy revisiting picture books or old favorites, and the younger grades always love a story. So, please don't hesitate to experiment with this unit.

Daily Assignment #8: Cautions

I've been thinking about the things I wished someone had told me to be cautious about when I first started teaching. I've created this list:

➢ Never release a student to a stranger. Make sure whoever is picking up a student has permission to do so.

➢ Touch or not touch. Be very careful. This is such a sensitive topic, particularly if you are a male teacher. There are students who may misinterpret a touch. There are also students who are tactile sensitive. I've always been a big hugger. However, there are students I am cautious about approaching. There are also students who might approach you and it is not comfortable. You need to make this call, be careful.

➢ On a similar note, if you find yourself alone with a student in the classroom, leave the door open. Consider stepping out in the hallway with the student.

➢ Continuing on this theme, DO NOT drive a student in your car. There are so many reasons not to do this and you probably know them. You may have the best intentions but if you were ever to get into an accident or a student accused you of something terrible your life would become a mess. Just don't do it.

➢ If you have a desk make sure it is facing the door so that you can see who is coming and going from your classroom.

➢ No matter how frustrating/disruptive a student maybe, never send him/her out of the room unescorted.

➢ Never leave your class unattended. Check to see what the policy at your school is for stepping out of the class for just a moment, e.g. bathroom. Some districts require a licensed teacher, in other districts it can be any staff member.

➤ Do not dispense medication, including vitamins, cough drops, ointments, ice. Check the schools policy on sending students to the nurse and procedures for medication. The school nurse should notify you of students with allergies or on medications. If a student may need an Epi-pen make sure the nurse instructs you on how to use it. For every field trip, or activity out of range of the nurse, make sure you have an emergency kit, especially the Epi-pen. Report accidents. Don't take any chances that it is nothing. Better to err on the side of caution than not. Notify parents. Parents do not like to hear about their child getting hurt 2 days later.

➤ Document everything. If there is something off for a student and you are not sure what to do about it speak with the school guidance counselor. Document, document. I continue to keep documentation of some students just in case.

➤ Know the school's Emergency Plan. I know of a school that did not have one until after a situation. As a result, there was chaos. Staff and students did not know where to go. Parents didn't know where to find their children. It was a chaotic mess.

➤ Preview videos that you are going to show to your class. I started a video o only to discover it had been taped over with an orgy scene from a Dracula movie. Talk about panicking.

➤ Candy as a reward. I am guilty of being a candy "Rewarder." I would give Swedish Fish or 1 Life Saver or 1 Hershey Kiss for various reasons, i.e. successful moments, when it would feel like the class was spiraling downw and just because. Simple treats are a quick reward, inexpensive, makes ki happy and can completely change the atmosphere in the classroom.   As become more health conscious, candy may not have a place in your classroom. Many teachers think it isn't a good idea to reward with candy a are concerned about parental disapproval. It might be a good idea to ask parents in a questionnaire at the beginning of the year whether they have issue with an occasional piece of candy. Of course, if there is a medical is you should be aware of that early on.

➤ Do not use sarcasm. Sarcasm is a "sharp, bitter, or cutting expression or remark; a bitter jibe or taunt, usually conveyed through irony or understatement". It is usually demeaning and cruel and has no place in a classroom. Teachers using sarcasm usually consider it a humorous and wit way to engage or reprimand a student or class. However, sarcasm creates negative interaction and environment. Students may react with an inappropriate response, which usually leads to negative consequences by tl teacher. There will always be one or more students who are worried that the might become the teachers next target for sarcasm. Again, don't use sarca in class, it hurts even if you don't think so.

➤ Do not say "Shut-up." Shut-up is an expression that used to be commonly used in classrooms. These days it is considered an offensive way to tell someone to be quiet. Using the expressions "please be quiet" or "please ca down" accomplishes the same thing without offending and making a studen defensive.

Other than that, please feel free to move about the classroom.

Daily Assignment # 9: Morning Meeting

Morning meeting is an important time for students. It is an opportunity for community building, instruction and the development of social skills. It can also set the tone for the day.

I would like to share with you the routine I used for Morning Meeting:

1. I would begin with an announcement, "We are ready to begin Morning Meeting. May I have everyone on the rug." (This was also a cue for parents to leave.)

2. Once the students had quickly settled down we would do a greeting. At the beginning of the year I would choose the greeting. After awhile a student would select the greeting.

3. Take the attendance. Students had to respond with "Here" or "Present". I did not allow "Yep" or any other responses.

4. Weather and temperature was reported by a student then graphed.

5. Day of the school year recorded in Arabic Numerals using a place value chart and then translated into Roman Numerals.

6. Schedule for the day and announcements.

7. Sharing with passing a "talking stick." Each student would say to the next student, "Would you like to share?" The next student would respond with, "Yes, thank you" if they were going to share and "No, thank you" if they were not going to share.

8. If a student was sharing they could only say 3 things. This helped the student who had difficulty in formulating their thinking in a concise way and it helped the student who could not come up with anything to begin. Some students practiced at home.

For example:
1. "One, I read a book about spiders."
2. "Two, I learned that the scientific name for spiders is arachnids."
3. " And three spiders have 8 legs."

9.   After the calling stick has made it around the circle, and if there is time, we would do questions and comments. I would ask if any student had a question or a comment. (Research has shown that high school students do not know the difference between comments and questions.) Students would raise their hands, say whom the question or comment was for, identify whether it was a question or comment and then say it. The student that it was directed to had to respond in an appropriate manner. They could say, "Thank you for your comment," or whatever else would be appropriate.

10. Meeting Adjourned

At this point you are probably thinking it must be getting dark or at least close to dismissal time. Actually, this all happens very quickly once you get the routine in place.

CHAPTER 2: THE HOW TO'S

Daily Assignment #10: Open House

Aaaahh, Open House. In the past, I would fear and dread Open House. I could easily stand in front of a room full of children and be comfortable. But put me in front of a room full of adults and I would have butterflies, my face would turn red, and all of a sudden the room would get hot. It wasn't pretty.

Parents have come to Open House to know about their child's day, what to do for birthdays, how to drop their child off in the morning and pick him/her up at the end of the day, what will parent- teacher communication look like, and the all important, homework schedule. Having said that, please know that they also want to see you. Knowing that, make sure you share something about yourself (where you grew up, your education, your family, your educational philosophy) as well as goals for the year. Make it brief.

Some teachers plan activities for parents to do, e.g. writing an encouraging letter to their child which can later be made into a bookmark for the child, making a clay figure which represents their child, doing a scavenger hunt by having them find things such as their child's work on the bulletin board, their child's desk, the books their child is using, and a message from their child.

Here is a format I used to avoid folks seeing my nervousness, which became a mainstay of my Open House presentations. A few days before the Open House take photos of the classroom, of the students during meeting time, reading, math, science, social studies, snack time, recess, etc... Include each child in at least one photo. (Parents will notice if their child is not in a photo.) Make a slide show or a power point presentation of the photos. For each slide describe what is happening. Make note cards for yourself, so that you are sure to hit all the important information.

1. *Elementary:* daily schedule, homework, grading, classroom rules, units of study.
2. *Middle/High School:* discipline policy, homework, grading, field trips, extracurricular activities

Leave about 15 minutes, at the end, for questions and comments. If you feel challenged by a question or comment, feel free to say, "I need to think about that and get back to you." Having said that, a question that always came up for me was one about homework. Make sure you know the district's, the school's, and your, homework policy.

Here are some other suggestions for designing Open House/Back to School Night:

- Consider sending student made invitations to parents.
- Dress professionally. I can't stress this enough. No mini-skirts, t-shirts, low-cut tops, etc…
- Prepare your room. Hang a "Welcome" sign outside the door, and be sure your name and the room number are prominently displayed.
- Have a sign-in sheet for parents.
- Have a handout with the agenda for the evening.
- Providing refreshments helps to make parents feel welcome.
- Freshen up your bulletin boards, and display a daily schedule.
- Set out sample textbooks.
- Be sure all desks and tables are clean.
- On each child's desk have a folder with samples of the student's work.
- Post student's work on bulletin boards. Make sure you have a sample from every student.
- Post photographs of students and activities throughout the room.
- Greet each parent at the door with a handshake and a smile, albeit a nervous one.
- Be sure every parent has a name tag (remember the last name of the parent may be different from the student's last name).
- Have a questionnaire for parents that includes what they would like to see their child improve in, something the teacher should know about the child, and the parent's perception of the child's best characteristics.
- Provide copies of the class/course syllabus.
- No matter what the questions or comments are, always think positive intentions.

Remember, the better prepared you are, the more professional you will look and feel. And don't forget to breathe and smile.

Daily Assignment #11: Birthday Celebrations

Handling students' birthdays can be a challenge. Parents' plans for their child's celebration in the classroom can be very different from what you are willing to handle. Invitations, alone can be a major problem. So, let me offer a strategy.

First, make it clear to parents that no invitations can be passed out in the classroom or outside the classroom door. I understand the reasoning for parents doing this—mostly for convenience because of not having mailing or email addresses. However, it can create chaos in the classroom. If one child is not included, the teacher must deal with the hurt feelings for the entire day. If a child loses their invitation, again, the classroom teacher must deal with the problem.

Second, let the parents know that all children will be treated the same for their birthdays. Parents may send in finger type snacks, e.g. munchkins, cookies, cupcakes, to be shared at snack time or sometime during the day. At that time the class will sing "Happy Birthday" to the child. Make it clear to parents that cakes, ice cream, drinks, party favors and, yes, even birthday parties, are unmanageable. They are time consuming, messy and can make other students feel uncomfortable about what their families can provide. It is also unnecessary for parents to be present during this time.

Notify all parents well in advance of the first celebration.

Daily Assignment #12: Holidays

For the month of December here is a list of some of the religious/ethnic holidays:

- *Ashura*, Islamic/Muslim
- *St. Nicholas Day*, International
- *Bodhi Day*, Buddhist
- *Virgin of Guadalupa*, Mexico
- *Santa Lucia Day*, Sweden
- *Las Posadas*, Mexico
- *Hanukkah*, Jewish
- *Christmas*, Christians, Roman Catholics, International
- *Kwanzaa*, African Americans

What should happen in the classroom during this holiday season?

Some teachers select several different holidays to teach about religious/ethnic traditions. Other teachers just share holiday traditions for one or two religions/ethnic groups. Another approach would to be to ask for parent volunteers to teach their religious/ethnic holiday traditions. Another approach might be to do nothing at all.

I've done it all. For me, I found the best approach was to ask for parent volunteers to come in and do a 30-40 minute presentation. If I didn't know the parent well, I would ask them to share with me their lesson plan in advance. In this way, I could help them with appropriateness for the age group and timing. The parents were always well prepared. It would be an amazing lesson and better than what I would have done.

There would be years when only one parent would come in, and I would need to teach 1or 2 more holidays. Then other years there might be 3 different parents who would come in to share 3 different holidays. If there were no volunteers then I would teach Hanukkah,
Christmas and Kwanzaa, or a holiday that reflected the population in the class.

Daily Assignment #13: "What Did You Do Over Vacation?"

A common question, that is asked of students, on the first day back from vacation is, "What did you do over vacation?" For some teachers it is the stem for a writing assignment or a class discussion. However, this question really separates the students into the "have's" and the "have not's". There are the students who travel to faraway lands, or go on a trip to Disney World, or go on amazing ski trips, or have a very busy social life with their peers. Then there are the students who stay at home because the parents need to work, and there is no money for lavish trips or even a dinner at McDonald's. Their social lives might be very limited or non-existent.

Let me share with you a different question for the first day back from vacation. Ask, "Who is someone you spent special time with over vacation and what was one thing you did with them, or why was the time special?" With this question every student will have something to write about or discuss. It levels the playing field.

On another note, don't be surprised to discover that your students have totally forgotten class routines. So, on Monday morning, you will need to review class procedures, routines, and expectations. Don't wait for an incident to happen and then reprimand the students. Be proactive and be prepared (and forewarned).

Daily Assignment #14: Extended Family Vacations/Trips

Over the years I found it challenging when a parent would come to me and say, "Eddie won't be in school next week. We're going on vacation. Please prepare work for him to do while we are away."

I totally understand parents traveling before or after the scheduled school vacations so that they may get that primo airfare. However, parents don't realize all the challenges and disruptions these extended trips/vacations have on the classroom and the teacher.

My response to these parents changed over the years. At the beginning of my career I would prepare all that work for the student to take on their vacation, only to have it returned to me unfinished or never returned at all. I don't think parents are aware of how much time it takes to prepare this work for their trip/vacation.

It was difficult to be pleasant to the habitual vacation family or the ones who would return all tanned and mellow and then expect me to catch their child up on everything the child had missed, or to the parent who brought their child to school straight from the airport where they had just returned from an 8-hour flight expecting me to deal with an exhausted child.

What I've learned:

Some trips/vacations are worth it, especially those in which the child would learn so much by the experience, such as a travel-learning trip/vacation.

Don't prepare the work for the student to take with them. Instead, tell the parent to have the student read 20-30 minutes each night, perhaps keep a reading journal. The parents should design 5-10 math problems each night for the child to solve. Also, have the student keep a journal, with photos or drawings, of their trip. Parents can also buy commercially produced workbooks.

Save all the work that is done during the student's absence. Give the work to the parents to do with the student at home and then return finished products for grading. Make sure to give the parent a deadline for the work to be returned.

It becomes increasingly more difficult for a student to miss school after grade 2, due to mandated testing.

Check to see what your district or school's policy is on this issue before you decide what you will be doing. If there isn't a policy, it would be beneficial for your school to establish one.

Daily Assignment #15: Notices/Homework Organizational Strategy

I would like to share with you an organizational strategy for sending School Notices and homework home.

The custodian at my school would always say he knew more about my classroom than parents because he always found the notices and homework on the floor. So, clearly I needed a new strategy for notices and homework assignments going home and coming back.

Have a pocket folder for each student, labeled with their name in one corner and "Homework and Notices" written on the center. On one of the pockets write "home" and on the other write "school." Any notices or homework assignments that were to go home, you guessed it, went on the "home" side. I think you can figure out the rest. Have a basket large enough to hold all folders near the door of the classroom, along with a class list. As students come in the next day, have them put their folders in the basket and check their names off the list. Simple, and yet, basic skills are being taught, e.g. organization, responsibility, to mention a few.

The first day you try this, there are several steps you will need to do. First, write a letter to parents letting them know about this strategy/routine. Then you must teach your students how to do the routine.
  Remember:
    1. Name it.
    2. State its purpose
    3. Model how it will look-- what the folder will look like, how they should take the papers out when they get home, how it will look when they complete their homework, making sure their name is on the papers, how to put papers back in the folder neatly, how to put the folder in the basket when they return to school, and how to check their name off the list.
    4. Have the students practice with a partner.
    5. Give feedback
    6. Practice

Now you are ready to send it home.

I know some of you are saying that this is way too elementary. Trust me, it isn't. Kids may roll their eyes and giggle, but they will remember.

Okay, on the next day, everybody gets it right! YEA!! You are awesome, which is probably what you're thinking. But in order to keep this routine successful, you must be tenacious about the steps.

Let's say it doesn't work the next day, what do you do. Re-teach. Sometimes it takes many re-teaching lessons, but if it is important to you, you need to be tenacious.

If you're not, the students perceive that you don't care. This is not a good precedent to set.

So, give it a lot of thought. Figure out if this is a strategy that is important to you and would make your life a little easier if you put in the effort now.

Daily Assignment #16: Homework

This is such a controversial topic. Parents want more and more homework for their children. Teachers spend a lot of time preparing and then grading homework. Is it necessary? I have read so many articles, which support the need for homework and then other articles which have said homework makes no difference in students' performances.

I would like to share with you my belief and practice in regard to homework. I believe, and please know that this is my belief based on 35 years of teaching experience and readings, that homework in the grades K-3 does not make a difference in a student's performance in the classroom. For students at these grade levels, I believe it is more important for them to read each night or to be read to. If you do decide to give homework at K-3 level, keep in mind that it should not take the child more than 10 minutes to do it. In grade 4, students should have no more than 15 minutes of math work and then 15-20 minutes of reading each night. In grades 5-6, students should have 50-60 minutes of homework each night. Harris M. Cooper, professor of education at Duke University and author of "The Battle Over Homework: Common Ground for Administrators, Teachers and Parents", says that 1 hour to 90 minutes of nightly homework for middle school students and 2 hours for high school students can be associated with greater academic achievement.

Homework should be purposeful, not busy work. This is going to take time and effort from the teacher. Also, grading of the homework should have meaning and help the student to move forward in their learning. Again, this will take time and effort from the teacher. Students know when they have been given busy work and when it is not going to make a difference in their final grade.

Another factor to consider is sometimes parents will do their child's homework. (Think-- Science Fair) If you notice a difference in a student's performance on their homework compared to their class work you might want to have a conversation with the parents. However, tread lightly if you approach the parents. Don't accuse the parent, merely share the data and explain you are trying to understand the discrepancy.

I hope this has given you something to think about as you plan that next homework assignment or think through your homework policy.

Daily Assignment #17: Homework Buddies

By now you probably know your students fairly well. This is a good time to pair students up as Homework Buddies. Explain to the students that they may exchange phone numbers and call each other in the evening if they are experiencing difficulty with a homework assignment. You can also use these partners to share homework assignments between them so they have to do only half the homework on occasion. Homework Buddies can also be used to check each other's answers the next day. This is a much more interesting way to go over homework and it engages the students in the process.

Make sure you are clear about the usage of Homework Buddies for your class. If, in setting the system up, you do not provide clarity on the difference between copying and helping you will end up with a mess.

Daily Assignment #18: Class Newsletter

A great way to communicate with parents on a weekly basis, and to have students reflect on major events each week, is to establish a weekly class newsletter. You're probably asking, "How on earth do I fit this into an already busy day?" Believe it or not, it can be very easy.

First, ask for parent volunteers. It doesn't have to be the same parent each week, but it does need to be on a consistent day and time. I've had one parent take on this responsibility for the whole year. I've also had 2, and some years 4, parents share this responsibility. When it's more than one parent, have them work out the weekly schedule among themselves.

Second, rotating through a class list, select 4 students a week to become reporters. Generating topics with the whole group helps to refresh everyone's memory. With the parent, the students select one topic each to write about. I restricted the topics to events within our class. That is to say, it couldn't be about events in their personal life or at recess or during specialist times. I also had the parent work with the students outside the classroom, e.g. hallway, cafeteria, library.

Third, you should write a message to the parents. It should include upcoming events, important information, e.g. thank you to all the reporters and the parent, progress within units of study, etc.

Fourth, the parent puts the newsletter together and makes all the copies. Remember to provide the parents with a model of what the final newsletter should look like.

You did it! And, you have created a strategy to involve parents in a non-threatening way.

Daily Assignment #19: Scheduling Parent Conferences

You have probably started to think about parent conferences. Scheduling is always a challenge. I recognize that schools may have a set way of conducting conferences. However, I would like to share with you a possible strategy for scheduling.

Send a schedule to parents, listing possible dates and times. A conference needs to be about 30 minutes long to be effective. If you have 25 students you should list about 33-35 possible dates and times. It is also considerate to have at least one late afternoon and a few times before school. These should be scheduled over a period of 2 months.

Have the parents select their 1st, 2nd, and 3rd choices. Circle the time that fits into the schedule, sign the original copy, and send it back home. Keep a master copy for yourself. Most teachers do this part through email. Keep in mind that not all families have Internet or check it frequently.

In the letter to parents explain the process of scheduling. Also, include what will happen if they miss the conference or need to reschedule. If parents miss the conference, and do not call, call them and say, "It is **unfortunate** that you missed your conference. I hope everything is okay. The next possible times for a conference are... (Provide 2-3 possible dates and times). Please let me know which one you will be attending."

Daily Assignment #20: Facilitating a Parent Conference

Let the conferences begin!

Make sure you do your homework before meeting with parents. If you are going to say something, whether it is academic or a reference to a social behavior, have evidence. I can't stress enough the importance of providing specific examples for whatever you say. Have assessment scores ready for academic references. When sharing social behaviors, good or bad, have specific examples with dates. Be prepared, but don't do a data-dumping meeting.

Begin the conference with, "What is your perception of how the beginning of the year is going for your child?" Instantly, you will find out the direction the conference will be taking. You will also discover if the parents have a realistic perception of the child's academic level and social behaviors.

I'm sure you've already heard this, but I'll say it again, share the positives first and then your concerns. Ask questions, e.g. "Who does your child consider his/her friends?" "What does your child do after school?" "Is there anything that I (teacher) should be aware of?"
To bring closure to the meeting, do a summary of the main points and of something that parents can do at home to support their child.

Lastly, take notes. Fill in the details after the parents leave. I discourage taking notes on a computer during the conference. As soon as you put the computer up, you have put a barrier between you and the parents. Parents, who have sat through conferences where the teacher took notes on the computer, said they felt the teacher was disconnected and that the clicking was annoying.

If you find that you are not able to cover all the information at this meeting, ask if you can schedule a follow-up meeting.

Relax. Smile. Recognize that this is a partnership. You need the parents to understand and support their child - and you.

Daily Assignment #21: LAFF Don't CRY

While researching the topic Active Listening, I came across this great strategy, which includes Active Listening, for facilitating parent-conferences, especially difficult ones. The acronym LAFF don't CRY, (McNaughty, Hamlin, McCarthy, Head-Reaves & Schreiner, 2008), stands for:

L Listen/empathize
A Ask questions
F Focus on the issue
F Find a 1st step

DON'T

C Criticize people who aren't present
R React hastily and promise something you can't deliver
Y Yakety-yak-yak off subject, e.g. talk about oneself

After reading about this strategy, I realized how many other scenarios this could be used in, e.g. staff meeting, family gatherings.

Daily Assignment #22: Calling Parents

When calling a parent begin by saying your name and whose teacher you are. Then say this is not an emergency, unless of course it is. If you get a voice mail just say you would like to speak with a parent and then leave your contact information. Do not leave a message if the student is in trouble. You don't know who else will be listening to the message and it can easily be deleted. Also, say that if you don't get a call back you will assume they didn't get the message and that you will try again.

Daily Assignment #23: Planning for a Substitute Teacher

It is inevitable, if it hasn't happened yet, that you will be absent. Do not stress over it. The students will be fine if you are out for a few days. It is much better for everyone if you stay home and take care of yourself than push yourself and, in the process, contaminate everyone.

Now, having said that, please know that I went to work many times feeling dreadful and, I am sure, with a fever. I went for many reasons: I thought the children would fall apart without me; I knew the room would fall apart without me; I didn't have plans for the next day. The fact is, when I was absent unexpectedly, everything was all right, albeit the children were glad when I returned.

Here is a strategy I adapted, which was very helpful. I call it Plan B, because Plan A, are those wonderful plans we do every day that anyone could teach.

Plan B: For each day of the week, have a 2-pocket folder. On one side put a typical daily schedule. On the other side have possible generic lessons, worksheets, and activities.
For example:
Literacy-- a short story with comprehension and recall questions, or a writing activity where students read 3/4 of the story and write a new ending.

Math--worksheets that review previously taught concepts, or activities/games students can do with partners or in teams.
Science--students choose an animal, from a list you have created, draw a sketch of it, and, using a descriptive graphic organizer, list characteristics selected from books, articles, and other resources, which have been set aside for this purpose.

Social Studies--with partners list as many countries, or states, or continents, (challenge-list capitals).

Also, in the folder, put the names of 2 or 3 students who would make good helpers for the sub.

By doing this now, in the unfortunate circumstance that you need to be absent, you can focus on getting better and not what is happening in your classroom and the substitute will thank you for being so well planned.

CHAPTER 3: CLASSROOM MANAGEMENT STRATEGIES

Daily Assignment #24: When Things Go Wrong, Whose Fault Is It?

Have you ever had a class where you dreaded the students coming in to the room? Or you feel all alone teaching in the front of the class, and you look out over a sea of confusion, fooling around, and/or disruptive behavior.

"Is it my fault? I've prepared, what I thought were great lessons. What happened? How did I lose them? Or are they just a bad class? They wouldn't get your lesson anyway." "They're not like this for Mr. B's math class. Why are they like this in my class? Maybe they just don't like me." These are all typical questions and comments when things are going badly.

This is a time to reflect on yourself as a teacher. It is easy to blame the students for management problems but a lot of times it is us, and we just don't see it.

Jon Saphier has addressed this topic, at length, in his book, _The Skillful Teacher_, Chapter 8, Discipline. You can actually download this chapter. You can also purchase the whole text.
http://www.rbteach.com/rbteach2/eBooks.asp
I highly recommend this book for your professional library.

Saphier lists 12 Causes of Disruptive or Inattentive Behavior:

- _Poor general management_
- _Inappropriate work_
- _Boring instruction_
- _Confusing instruction_
- _Unclear standards, expectations, and consequences_

- *Student ignorance on how to do the expected behaviors*
- *A need for fun and stimulation*
- *Value and culture clashes*
- *Internal physical causes*
- *External physical causes*
- *Extraordinary emotional baggage*
- *Student's sense of powerlessness.*

I'm not going to go into detail on each of these because I really want to encourage you to read this chapter yourself. However, you can get a general idea of what you need to think about while reflecting by just reading the list.

If you are still struggling with what might be the causes, during reflection, you might want to ask a colleague to come in, observe, collect data and share it with you. Mr. B might be the perfect person.

Daily Assignment #25: Time-Out

There are times when a student needs to be removed from a situation and have a time-out. It may mean the student is seated out in the hallway or a designated place in the classroom. I prefer a designated place in the classroom for safety reasons.

Make sure the student knows why they are having a time-out. Make the explanation brief. This is not the time to lecture the student.

For younger students give them a 3 minute egg timer, which helps them to understand that there is an end to the time-out. Also, it puts them in charge of the time. In this way, the teacher is empowering the student to not only be in charge of the time, but to be in charge of their behavior. When the 3 minutes are up the student may return to the group quietly. Welcome the student back. If possible, ask the student to say one thing that indicates that they are ready to return.

This strategy sends the message to the student that they are not a bad person they just need time to gain control and to be able to behave appropriately. Avoid excessive use of time-out. Time-outs should not exceed 5-10 minutes, for younger students. Older students' time-outs should not exceed 15 minutes or until they are 21.

Each step for Time-Out needs to be taught.

1. Name it
2. State the purpose
3. Model

If the same student is repeatedly having time-outs clearly, the strategy does not work for that student.

Some teachers may have the student put their head down on their desk.

Daily Assignment #26: Annoying Classroom Behaviors

We all have experienced those annoying classroom behaviors by our students, e.g. chatting, sharpening pencils at inopportune moments, not cooperating within a group, etc.

What to do...

1. Set up a group contract, using classroom rules that have been established.
2. Review the rules, weekly or daily, until the students can successfully adhere to them.
3. Use direct and specific reprimands, "Stop talking and work on your math problems, please."
4. Frequently give praise to the whole class, "Thank you for working so quietly." "Thank you for cleaning your area so quickly."
5. Be proactive. If you see a student becoming distracted intervene quickly. "Harry, you with us?"
6. Use the "Look", (Daily Assignment #93: Messages Teachers Send Through Body Language).
7. Frequently circulate around the room.

For the student who continues to have difficulty, designing an individual contract maybe necessary.

Daily Assignment #27: Getting Students' Attention and Keeping It

We all have so many strategies for getting students' attention and keeping it. It would be great if you could sit with your colleagues and list the many strategies used. Most teachers are not even cognizant of how many strategies they use within a 30-minute block of time.

Here is a list of some attention strategies that I have used and some I know other teachers have used:

- Clapping patterns
- Switching lights on and off
- Hands on head
- Stop and Stare
- Name- dropping
- Reprimand
- Voice variety
- Ringing a bell or chimes
- Hand signal
- Standing close to disruptive student
- Using a threat
- Removing student
- Knock it off/stop moves
- Whole group: "Okay folks, let's settle down."
- Individual: "Richard, you need to focus on..."
- Using a student's name in an example
- Calling on a student
- Music
- Being dramatic
- Humor
- Questions
- Make a student a helper

After reading the list of strategies above, I hope you will take an opportunity and list strategies you use. Ask a colleague to come in and check off or write down, which ones you use during a lesson or period.

Then reflect on the data. If you find that you are using more "Knock it off" moves than engaging moves, consider this an opportunity to experiment with new more positive strategies to getting student's attention.

Pre-Alert is an effective attention strategy for students who have difficulty speaking or formulating thoughts, or who are not quite part of the classroom and become isolates. Pre-Alert gives that student a heads up, time to prepare, to take a deep breathe, think about what they are going to say, and really pay close attention to what the teacher is saying and doing.

Example:
While reading a story aloud, the teacher pauses and says, "Mark, I'm going to be calling on you in a few minutes, so make sure you are paying attention."

Pre-Alert is also an effective strategy for the student who is not paying attention or who is fooling around. You're letting them know you are going to be calling on them so they better pay attention.

Here's the tough part, remembering that you gave a pre-alert to a particular student and then going back to them.

Daily Assignment #29: Eyes in the Back of Your Head

We are amazing people. We notice things going on all over our classroom. When working with a small group, we know what Johnny is doing over by the door and what Sasha and Claudia are doing at their seats. We can tell Julia to get back on task by using a signal and give permission to Tim to go to the bathroom. Amazing!

All of these are management strategies called "Overlapping". It is a term created by Jacob Kounin, a classroom behavioral theorist. In Kounin's book, _Discipline and Group Management in Classrooms,_ he states "overlapping is the ability to attend to two issues at the same time."

I believe we actually attend to many more than 2 issues at a time. We are masters at doing this.

So, the next time you notice a child off task and say something to them and then turn and finish a lesson with a group, say "Aha, I just did 'Overlapping.'"

Daily Assignment #30: Downtime--Be Prepared

We all have those moments when something happens unexpectedly, downtime occurs, students have nothing to do. It can be very scary, especially if you haven't developed a repertoire of strategies to fill those moments.

Let me give you some examples of what I mean: The music teacher is behind schedule and your class is waiting in the hallway. Or the school nurse is checking all the students' hearing and vision, and you can't teach a lesson because half the class is at the nurse's office and the other half is with you. Or it is photo day, and the class is lined up waiting for their turn, which feels like forever. Or some students have finished their work, and others are still working. Or it's dismissal time and buses are late. The list goes on and on. Sound familiar? What is amazing is that these can all happen within one day.

So, what should you do? Keep on hand ideas to fill these moments. Examples: Fast Math, Simon Says, Hangman, Math Facts; name states, capitals, countries, rivers, baseball/football teams, famous pairs, e.g. Bert and Ernie, Otis and Milo, Anthony and Cleopatra, Adam and Eve, songs, e.g. Head, Shoulders, Knees and Toes; skip counting, telephone, spelling challenge. Notice some of these are content related, others are fun and just to get through the moment.

Take a moment and collect a few ideas to build your repertoire. Check in with colleagues, find out what they are doing and exchange ideas.

Daily Assignment #31: Rock/Paper/Scissors

I'm sure you remember this game from childhood. Did you know that children in Japan are taught this game to solve some problems, such as who gets the ball first?

After witnessing the effectiveness of this strategy myself, I decided to implement it in my classroom. I must say it eliminated my having to deal with a lot of little things that might have otherwise been taking up valuable teaching time.

Students used Rock/Paper/ Scissors to solve ---- who got the coveted seat, who were the captains for games at recess, who passed out papers, who used certain art supplies first, and the list goes on. It was wonderful to see the students take total responsibility in solving problems that had the potential to become a major distraction from learning.

If you decide to experiment with this strategy make sure you:
1. Name it
2. State what it is for
3. Describe how to do it
4. Model
5. Students practice
6. Give feedback
7. Practice more

Tidbit: I had the students stand back to back. Some students would hesitate just long enough to see what the other student was going to do.

Daily Assignment #32: "I" Message

The "I" Message is an effective management strategy. Thomas Gordon coined the phrase "I" Message, in 1960.
It consists of 3 parts:

    a. A non-blameful description: When you interrupt my teaching...

    b. The effect of the behavior on you: I feel frustrated...

    c. What you would like to happen next: I would like you to raise your hand if you want to speak.

Using this language takes the "you" out of the message and makes it nonjudgmental. You are stating facts.

Examples:

1. Jack leaves the lab table and leaves the materials out.

    "Jack, when you leave the materials out,
    I feel afraid that the materials will be broken.
    Please put the materials away."

2. Maria finishes eating her snack and leaves, leaving behind her trash.

    "Maria, when you leave trash on the table,
    I feel frustrated because I have to clean it up.
    Please put your trash in the wastebasket after eating."

These 3 key phrases can act as a guide:

    1. When you...
    2. I feel...
    3. I would like...

Daily Assignment #33: Energizers

Energizers are get up and move activities that can take 60 seconds, or longer, to do. They are a quick way of getting the blood from the butt back up to the brain. Energizers can also be a community building activity. Students need them, particularly if they have been sitting through a sit-and-get instructional period. It doesn't matter the age group, we all need a stand and stretch moment. Think about it. Have you ever been in a class where you have been unable to maintain your attention on the instructor because you just need to move around? As gifted and exciting as we are as teachers, believe me, your students have tuned you out as well during instruction. So, get them up and moving. You'll get more out of them when they return to their seats.

Here are a few examples of quick energizers:

1. **"My Bonnie Lies Over the Ocean"**: Everyone begins by being seated. Then begin singing the song. Every time a "b" word is said either stand or sit. So, for the first "b" word, (Bonnie), everyone stands. Then for the second "b" word, again Bonnie, everyone sits. Continue with this pattern. If it has been done correctly, everyone will end up seated.

2. **Simon Says**: I know you all know this one. However, let me offer this simpler version--only do head, shoulder, waist, and knees. Also, no one is ever out. Just smile and keep going. This way keeps everyone engaged and no one is sitting out, and possibly being disruptive.

3. **Simply stand and stretch**.

4. **Zip, Zap, Zop**: Stand in a circle. One person has a Nerf ball or beach ball. They make eye contact with someone across the circle and say "Zip", and throw the ball at that person. That person makes eye contact with someone else across the circle, say "Zap", and throws the ball at that person. Then that person makes eye contact across the circle, says "Zop", and throws the ball at that person. Then it all begins again. The pace can be quite fast. They cannot throw it at a person beside them. They have to throw the ball across the circle.

5. **Catch Me If You Can**: Players should be paired up. All players divide into two lines, facing in shoulder to shoulder, with partners facing each other. Participants should be given approximately 30 seconds to look at their partners, taking in all details about the individual. The leader then instructs the two lines to turn and face away from the center.

One or both lines have 15-20 seconds to change something about their appearance (i.e. change a watch to different wrist, unbutton a button, remove a belt, etc.). The change must be discrete, but visible to the partner. The players again turn in to face each other and have 30 seconds to discover the physical changes that have been made. Players get to interact with each other and have fun!

6. **Sing "Head, Shoulders, Knees and Toes"** with actions.

7. **Left-Right Alphabet**: Write the alphabet on large chart paper. Underneath each letter of the Alphabet put an L or R.
A B C D E F G H ...
L L R L R R R L...
Do a random sequence of L's and R's. Students stand and sing the alphabet and, as they do so, they raise either the left arm or right arm depending on the letter. This is great fun, as well as challenging.

8. **Think-Pair-Share**: When sharing students must stand, make eye contact with someone across the room, walk to them, and then share.

Daily Assignment #34: Preparing Students for Transitions

It is important to help students' transition from one activity to the next. Abruptly ending an activity that students are engaged in and then quickly moving them to the next activity creates confusion and anxiety.

For example: The students are doing math activities that are very engaging. Abruptly, the teacher stands and says, "Put the math materials away and take out your writing folder."

The teacher has just interrupted the students' learning. What was happening in the math activity may have been a pivotal point in understanding a concept for a student. They have been jerked out of one activity and then thrust into another one.

Here is another example of a jerk and thrust transition that I was guilty of doing more than once: The students are really focused and engaged in a writing assignment. I look up and notice it is time for gym. I say, "Quick, put your pencils down and get in line for gym."

Some teachers, give a "warning" that the next activity will happen in a few minutes. The word "warning" carries a negative meaning; something bad is about to happen. I prefer using the word "notice". It sounds less threatening, e.g. "This is a 5 minute notice until gym."

Setting a timer is an easy and inexpensive way to not only help the teacher to stay on time but to also help the students stay focused. Using a timer guarantees that the class will be at specialist on time or will transition at the right time. I also set it to remind me to pick the students up from specialist on time. Students can have the responsibility of the timer. Have one student set the timer for the length of the activity, lesson, or whatever. Set it for 5 minutes before the transition, so students will know how much time they have to clean up and prepare for the next activity. You will be amazed at how smoothly transitions will occur.

Daily Assignment #35: Physical Movement of Students

Physical movement of students within the classroom during transitions can be a challenge. We do this in many different ways throughout the day. It can happen smoothly or be absolutely chaotic. If a teacher says, "Line up for lunch," chances are chaos will result. Some students will get in line, some will chat, some will start fooling around, and some may never make it to lunch. Movement within an activity or lesson or after an activity or lesson is also a crucial matter. A lot of instructional time can be lost during these movements. Therefore, we need a repertoire of strategies for dividing and moving the "herd" in a quick and efficient ways.

Here is a list of a few strategies:

1. By individual names'

2. Alphabetical order

3. Reverse alphabetical order (beginning with Z)

4. Table groups

5. Teams

6. Partners

7. Teacher begins with one student, then that student selects the next student, and so on. Be careful with this one. You don't want to create an isolate in the class.

8. Style of shoes- tie, slip-on, velcro

9. Style of shirtsleeves- long, short, none

10. Shirt style- designs, stripes, solids, colors, "if you have on blue..."

11. Pets- "if you have a dog..." or "if you have 2 pets"

12. Assigning jobs for groups while other students get seated or line up

13. Having supplies/materials in easily accessible places so that congestion doesn't occur

14. Pacing of activities and lessons e.g., one group moves from one activity to another before the next group switches

It is amazing to think of all the decisions we make as teachers and these strategies are just a few more.

Daily Assignment #36: Blurt Alert

Have you ever noticed some students who are constantly blurting out the answer without raising their hand or waiting for their turn?

There are many ways to address the problem of students blurting out the answers. One way would be to ignore the student. Another way would be to praise the student who does raise their hand.

Here's a list of other possible strategies:

- Give the blurter a specific number of chips for the day/period. Each time the student blurts out the teacher takes a chip. Once the chips are used up the student can no longer speak. There should be consequences if they do continue. Hopefully, the student will recognize how often they do blurt out and will begin to stop.

OR

- As the student blurts out give them a chip. Count up the chips at the end of the day/period. Establish a goal. Have the student work towards reducing the quantity each day and striving for the goal. Provide a reward when they have reached a goal.

OR

- Red Hand Alert (Excerpted from the book, Class Cards.)
Red Hands are cut from red construction paper. They are kept on the teacher's desk. Whenever a student blurts out an answer or response when it is inappropriate to do so, stop everything, pick up one of the Red Hands, and extend it to the blurter. He/She is then required to write their name and the date on the hand. The hand is then dropped into a plastic container that holds the hands. At the end of the week, one of the students goes through the container and records on a grade sheet-- using a simple stick tally--the number of hands each student received. The students with the most Red Hands have them stapled to Student Bulletins, which are then sent home.

It's this type of specific, goal-oriented communication that really gets results. We're not saying that the child is completely irresponsible. He/She just needs to exercise a bit more self- control.

Note for middle school teachers: Pass out red squares instead of hand-cut outs. This will reduce the possibility that your students might see this technique as being a "baby school" thing.

Green Hands are given out at the end of the week to students who had gone through the week without receiving a Red Hand. The Green Hands are taken home, signed by one of the parents, returned to class, and then dropped in a little clear plastic container. During the week draw out Green Hands--one each day--and give the student some type of little prize, e.g. a Jolly Rancher, permission to leave a few minutes early for lunch, etc.

Helping the student who blurts out to recognize their behavior is the key.

Daily Assignment #37: Using Music in the Classroom

Using classical music in the classroom has many benefits for students. There is a phenomenon called the "Mozart Effect" where college students had "enhanced spatial task performance" after listing to Mozart's music. On the other side, there are studies that say listening to Mozart makes no difference in student performance. I found using music in the classroom helped to motivate students to complete their work. I also used music during transitions, clean up and at any other times at which it felt appropriate. Using music in the classroom can make learning more enjoyable.

If you decide to use music in your classroom, classical music is best. Having said that, I recommend that you match the music to the age group of your students and current tasks. Whatever music you select should be an instrumental. Otherwise the students will focus on the lyrics. And it should not be any faster than a heartbeat. If you play fast music you will find that the students become hyped up instead of calmer. Also, you will find that the students will need a variety of instrumental music to keep them engaged. Playing music from different genres is a great way for students to learn about various types of music, not to mention culture and history.

My class had a theme song it was Kermit the Frog's song "Rainbow Connection", as sung by Sarah McLachlan. I also taught with a middle school math teacher who played "Hit the Road Jack", by Ray Charles at the end of every class. In fact, the 8th graders sang this song to him, in honor of his retirement, at their graduation ceremony. It was fantastic!

Suggested music:

Music for visualization and imagery:

Beethoven	*Symphony No. 6* (Pastorale)
Debussy	*The Sea; Nocturnes*
Liszt	*Hungarian Rhapsodies*
Mozart	*Piano Concerto No. 21*
Tchaikovsky	*Romeo and Juliet Overture*
Vivaldi	*The Four Seasons*

Music for focusing:

J.S. Bach	*Brandenburg Concertos; The Well-Tempered Clavier*
Brahms	*Violin Concertos*
Handel	*Water Music*
Telemann	*Concerto for 3 Violins and Orchestra*

Music for calming:

Bruch	*Scottish Fantasy*
Copland	*Quiet City; Appalachian Spring*
Debussy	*Clair de Lune*
Wagner	*Evening Star*

Music to relieve tension:

J.S. Bach	*Air on a G String*
Debussy	*Images*
Faure	*Piano music*
Giuliani	*Guitar Concerto*
Pachelbel	*Canon in D*

Music for celebration:

Beethoven	*Chorale Fantasy for Piano, Chorus & Orchestra*
	Grand March

Verdi

Music for clean-up:

Brahms	*Symphony No. 3*
Berlin	*Any select*
Dvorak	*Cello Concert*

From: <u>Accelerated Learning With Music: A /Trainer's Manual</u>, Terry Wyler Webb with Douglas Webb

One more tidbit---when you are ready to turn the music off, do not just turn the music off, slowly lower the volume until it is off.

Daily Assignment #38: Put Downs/Push Ups

Put Downs/Push Ups is an effective management strategy, which I learned from a 4th grade teacher. Make a large T-chart, title one column Put Downs and the other Push Ups. As a whole class, brainstorm what Put Downs look and sound like. Do the same for Push Ups.

Put Downs	Push Ups

The brainstorming may not be an easy task for students. They seem to easily come up with the Put Downs but have difficulty coming up with Push Ups. This is an opportunity to teach students how to take a negative statement/comment or action, and turn it into a positive one. Take time to teach new vocabulary which will help students think of new ways of saying something more positive.

Post the chart in the classroom in a very visible place as a reminder of what they should be saying and what they shouldn't be saying. When a negative comment is said, the students can refer to the chart for rephrasing into a positive statement/comment or action.

Implementing this strategy will change the behavior in the classroom.

Students will work better as a community and, in general, be more respectful. It will take work and consistency to be effective. But then, again, everything that is important does.

CHAPTER 4: BASIC BACKGROUND KNOWLEDGE

Daily Assignment #39: 7 Steps for Effective Instruction

Researchers have found that to make instruction more effective:

- *Begin a lesson stating the objectives.*
- *Do a quick review of previous learning.*
- *Present new material in small steps and have students practice after each step.*
- *Give clear and detailed instruction and explanations.*
- *Provide a lot of practice.*
- *Check for understanding.*
- *Provide feedback and corrections.*

This does take time. But you will notice an increase in students' understanding. So, it is worth the effort.

Daily Assignment #40: Designing a Unit of Study

Designing a unit of study can be very overwhelming. Let me break it down in to more manageable steps for you.

1. *Begin with researching the topic. Keep a list of resource materials. Make sure to use the latest resources on the topic. Become knowledgeable.*
2. *Decide what it is that students are to know and to be able to do by the end of this unit.*
3. *How will learning be assessed and how frequently?*
4. *Do anActivator with the students to find out how much they already know about the topic and any misconceptions or confusions they may have on the topic.*
5. *Using the data from the Activator start designing the unit.*

Questions to ask while planning the unit:

- *What is the time span for this unit?*
- *How frequently will I be teaching this unit, e.g., every day, every other day? How many lessons will I need?*
- *Knowing the objectives, what will each lesson include?*
- *What thinking skills should be included?*
- *In thinking about each lesson, what effective strategies can be included to meet the needs of all my students?*
- *What strategies can be used to include the visual, auditory, and kinesthetic learners?*
- *What projects or activities, which will promote understanding, can be incorporated into the lessons? Include a rubric*
- *What summarizers should be used?*

As you teach this unit keep notes on how things are going. In that way, when you teach this unit again, you will remember the stumbling blocks and the successes. Don't worry if you don't get everything in the first time. Just keep building on what you have each year. Also, keep samples of students' work for reference, particularly when using a rubric.

Daily Assignment #41: Framing Learning

Framing learning means letting the students know what the objectives of the lesson are, using kid friendly language.

Example:

- The objective: *"You will know and be able to use question marks at the end of an 'asking' sentence."*
- Stating the purpose: *"You will be able to write an 'asking' sentence."*
- How they will learn it-procedural: *"Here is the Sequence of the Lesson."*
- How they will know they know it: *"You will be making "telling" sentences into "asking" sentences."*
- How you, the teacher, will know they know it: Assessment

Framing learning can be done verbally or written, e.g. chart, smart board.

Vocabulary for Framing Learning:

Draw, State, Record, Recognize, Identify, Sort, Describe, Select, Present, Locate Information from Text, Decide, Discuss, Define, Classify, Explain how, Devise, Calculate, Interpret, Construct, Clarify, Plan, Predict, Conclude, Solve, Determine the Key points from..., Formulate, Explain why, Use the pattern to..., Reorganize, Explain the differences between..., Make connections between..., Use the idea of ... to..., Use a model of... to..., Provide evidence for…, Evaluate the evidence for...

Framing learning provides students with a road map to their learning. By framing learning, students won't be sitting in front of you trying to figure out what the lesson is all about, or playing "Guess What's on the Teacher's Mind".

Daily Assignment #42: Writing Objectives

When I started teaching, writing the objectives for a lesson was something you did when you were student teaching. Now, objectives for lessons are required. Some districts/schools require teachers to post the objectives in the classroom for a lesson so that students understand what they are to know and be able to do by the end of class. My experience, not only as a student, but also as a beginning teacher was more of "guess what's on the teacher's mind." My instruction was also activity- driven, meaning I really wasn't sure what the students were supposed to know or be able to do but I sure knew they were having fun.

Since those beginning years, I have learned a great deal about understanding objectives of lessons and how to articulate them. Let me share with you an <u>abbreviated</u> version of how to write objectives.

First, look at your lesson and decide what it is you want students to know and to be able to do as a result of the learning experience.

Second, write--"Students will know... and be able to..."

Objectives should be specific, observable, measurable, and contain verbs, such as the ones listed below:

Objective language:

Cite, Choose, Define, Label, List, Locate, Match, Name, Arrange, Classify, Describe, Diagram, Draw, Explain, Identify, Apply, Demonstrate, Illustrate, Interpret, Predict, Categorize, Differentiate, Predict, Conclude, Critique, Support, Evaluate, Contrast, Interpret, Solve, Prove, Research, Write, State, Discuss, Estimate, Summarize, Analyze.

There are many more verbs that can be used to describe what students will know and be able to do. These are just a few.

Examples:

1. Students will know and be able to state five facts about the planet Mars.
2. Students will know how to solve an algorithm in division with 5-digit numbers and be able to solve 10 division algorithms.
3. Students will be able to define what a persuasive essay is and write to write a 3 paragraph persuasive essay.
4. Students will know 3 shapes and 4 colors and be able to use the vocabulary in describing a picture.
5. Students will know how to summarize a story and be able to use a summarizing graphic organizer.

Of course, you need to translate objectives into kid-friendly language. For younger students, giving the objective in verbal form is more appropriate than writing on a chart/smart board. For older students, posting the objectives and verbally giving them is important.

Your students will pay much more attention to the lesson because they know what they will need to know and be able to do after the lesson. It is so much better to have them have this information beforehand than to have them sitting in front of you trying to guess what's on your mind.

Daily Assignment #43: Thinking Skills, What Are They?

We hear so much about teaching "Thinking Skills." I'm sure everyone has heard of Bloom's Taxonomy of Thinking Skills: http://eduscapes.com/tap/topic69.htm.

There is also Deborah Burn's Taxonomy of Thinking Skills: http://www.gifted.uconn.edu/sem/typeiips.html?

Bottom line, this is my definition: "Thinking Skills" are the higher level learning objectives that teachers design for students within a lesson. Wow, that was a mouthful.

Let me give you some examples of what this means:

Objective for a literature lesson: *Students will know and be able to identify 5 characteristics of the main character in the novel To Kill A Mockingbird, by completing a Descriptive Graphic Organizer.*

  *The "Thinking Skill" is an Analytical Reasoning Skill: Identifying Characteristics (Bloom's). The graphic organizer provides a visual tool for the student.

Objective for a math lesson: *Students will know and be able to categorize a group of 10 objects according to attributes.*

   * The "Thinking Skill" is, again, an Analytical Reasoning Skill: Categorizing (Bloom's).

Objective for a social studies lesson: *Students will know and be able to brainstorm 8 possible reasons people have migrated to the U.S.A.*

   *The "Thinking Skill is a Creativity Skill: Brainstorming and a Critical Thinking Skill: Deductive Thinking.

Most lessons have thinking skills embedded within them. Being cognizant of the importance of "Thinking Skills" during planning is essential. You might want to take the opportunity to reflect on previously taught lessons and highlight the "Thinking Skills."

If you discover that your lessons do not include a "Thinking Skill", it is time to deliberately include them and teach them within your lesson designs. Take a look at the links included in the first paragraph to help your planning.

Daily Assignment #44: Multiple Intelligences

We're all familiar with Howard Gardner's work on multiple intelligences. Gardner has identified 8 intelligences, which are listed below:

Spatial
Linguistic
Logical-mathematical
Bodily-kinesthetic
Musical
Interpersonal
Intrapersonal
Naturalistic

So, what does this mean for a classroom teacher? Well, it means that as we plan our lessons we need to think about these intelligences and how we might incorporate them into our lesson.

For example:

Spatial--use graphics, drawings, maps, pictures, visualizations, videos, art, graphic organizers, illustrations, smart boards

Linguistic--speaking, dialogues, debates, plays, narratives

Logical-Mathematical--reasoning, deductive and inductive logic, facts, data, organizing, analyzing, assessments, outlines, timelines, analogies, patterns, problem solving, formulas

Bodily-Kinesthetic--art, activity, action, hands-on experiments, drama, sports, manipulatives, touch, field trips, role playing, learning centers, labs, games, cooperative learning activities

Musical--music, rhythm, pacing, chorus, jingles, background music, songs

Interpersonal--interactions, share, talk, socialize, clubs, working in pairs, group work, think-pair-share

Intrapersonal--solitude, think time, reflection journals, self-assess, set goals, write, introspection, independent assignments

Naturalist--exploring nature, outdoor education, observation, identification, classifying, categorizing, living things, field trips, ecology studies

As you plan a lesson for next week, try to include, within that lesson, at least 2 strategies to address 2 different multiple intelligences.

When planning a unit of study, include as many of the intelligences as possible. You and the students will meet with greater success.

Daily Assignment #45: Models of Teaching---An Introduction

In the text, _The Skillful Teacher_, by Saphier, Haley-Speca, Gower, a model of teaching is defined as "a pattern of instruction that is recognizable and consistent." Models of teaching teach a particular kind of thinking.

Joyce and Weil, Models of Teaching, established 4 categories of models.

> _Behavior Modification_
> _Information Processing_
> _Social Interaction_
> _Personal_

An example of an Information Processing Model is Hilda Taba's Inductive Reasoning/Thinking. This model was designed to improve the students' ability to handle information. There are 3 categories and 9 phases to this model:

1. Present the data to the students or collect it from them.
> _Phase One_: Enumeration and listing
> _Phase Two_: Grouping
> _Phase Three_: Labeling, Categorizing

2. Present a focus statement and have the students classify the data based on common attributes.
> _Phase Four_: Identifying Critical Relationships
> _Phase Five_: Exploring Relationships
> _Phase Six_: Making Inferences

3. Apply the concepts that emerge, explore relationships, make predictions.
> _Phase Seven_: Predicting Consequences, Explaining Unfamiliar Phenomena, Hypothesizing
> _Phase Eight:_ Explaining and/or Supporting the Predictions and Hypotheses
> _Phase Nine_: Verifying the Prediction

Lesson Using Inductive Model:

The teacher will begin by asking the students to think of anything that comes to mind regarding the reasons for the war of 1898. As they call out their ideas the teacher will write them on the board.

The teacher will then ask each student why they chose what they called out.

The teacher will then ask them to get into their pre-assigned groups and brainstorm about which ideas belong together in a grouping. The teacher will then write those groups on the board, going with the most prominent and again ask why the students chose as they did.

The teacher will now ask the student groups to label or put those groups into a particular category. The teacher will write all their ideas on the board and they may vote on the most prominent.

The teacher will now again ask why they chose as they did drawing on their responses to ask further questions.

The teacher will then tell the class that they have essentially outlined an essay listing the key factors leading to the war of 1898 and may use this method individually to accomplish an essay or to clarify their thoughts on a subject.

Daily Assignment #46: Model of Teaching---Concept Attainment

To recap, models of teaching is defined as "*a pattern of instruction that is recognizable and consistent*" and teaches a particular kind of thinking.

I would like to share with you another effective model of teaching entitled Concept Attainment. This instructional strategy is based on Jerome Bruner's work. In Concept Attainment students compare and contrast examples that contain attributes of a group with examples that do not contain those attributes and then form a concept definition of the group. Concept Attainment can be used to teach almost any concept in any subject.

To do Concept Attainment the teacher selects a concept and develops positive and negative examples. The teacher then shows the students one positive example and one negative example. The students work to develop a concept definition. The teacher gives additional examples. With each additional example, the students revisit their concept definition to see if it still fits. Students should process their concept definition and evaluate the accuracy.

Proper Nouns	Not Proper Nouns
Exeter St.	road
Florida	state
Richard	man
Japan	country

Math Example: *(from "Instructional Strategies Online")*

First, choose a concept to develop, i.e. Math facts that equal 10.
Then begin by making list of both positive "yes" and negative "no"
examples: The examples are put onto sheets of paper or flash cards.
Positive Examples: Positive examples contain attributes of the
concept to be taught; i.e. 5+5, 11-1, 10X1, 3+4+4, 12-2, 15-5,
(4X2)+2, 9+1
Negative Examples: For examples choose facts that do not have 10
as the answer; i.e. 6+6, 3+3, 12-4, 3X3, 4X4, 16-5, 6X2, 3+4+6,
2+(2X3), 16-10

Set up a chart, at the front of the room, with two columns - one
marked YES and the other marked NO.

Present the first card by saying, "This is a YES." Place it under the
appropriate column. i.e. 5+5 is a YES
Present the next card and say, "This is a NO." Place it under the NO
column. i.e. 6+6 is a NO
Repeat this process until there are three examples under each
column.

Ask the class to look at the three examples under the YES column
and discuss how they are alike; i.e. 5+5, 11-1, 2X5) Ask "What do
they have in common?"

Ask the students to decide if the next 6 examples—3 each positive
and negative- go under YES or NO.
At this point, there are 6 examples under each column. Several
students will have identified the concept, but it is important that they
not tell it out loud to the class. They can, however, show that they
have caught on by giving an example of their own for each column.

At this point, the examples are student-generated.

Ask the class if anyone else has the concept in mind. Students who
have not yet defined the concept are still busy trying to see the
similarities of the YES examples.

Place at least three more examples under each column that are student-generated.

Discuss the process with the class.

Once most students have caught on, they can define the concept.

When the students have pointed out that everything under the YES column has an answer of 10, then print a new heading at the top of the column--10 Facts. Then print a new heading for the NO column -- Not 10 Facts.

Math Example by Andrea Johnson: Polygons:

Using an overhead, a T-chart is drawn on a transparency.
In one column are examples of polygons
In the other are non-polygons
Sticky notes cover all examples.
One example from each column is shown
Together the students design a concept definition.
Another example is shown and the concept definition is evaluated.
Continue this process.
Evaluate the final concept definition. Does it hold true?

Daily Assignment #47: Model Of Teaching-- Inquiry Model

The Inquiry Model is a strategy created by Dr. J. Richard Suchman to help students to develop the skill of asking questions which seek answers that will enable them to solve a discrepant event or situation. Most educators associate this model to math and science; however, it can be used in all content areas.

Steps for the Inquiry Model:
- The teacher selects a discrepant event or situation, which has been researched, to present to the students.

- The students formulate questions which the teacher can answer with a yes or no response. The students must construct the questions in such a way that will give them the information they need to solve the discrepant event or situation.

- The students create a hypothesis. The students organize the information and assess the hypothesis.

- The students reflect on their inquiry process, and how it can be improved.

Examples:
Essay writing: Two students in a 9th grade English class wrote an essay of about 300 words on "Social Justice". Both had good ideas and expressed themselves accurately as far as grammar and vocabulary were concerned. However, one received an "A" while the other student got a "C". Why should there have been such a big difference between their grades?

Science: The first law of motion states that an object at rest tends to remain at rest and an object in motion tends to stay in motion. Why?

Social Studies: Han Chinese women from the 10th century until 1949 had tiny, deformed feet. Non- Han Chinese women did not. Why did Han Chinese women have deformed feet? Why did non-Han Chinese women have normal feet?

There are so many more examples, in all content areas, where the Inquiry Model would be a good match. So, keep it in mind when planning a lesson.

Daily Assignment #48: Rubrics

Heidi Goodrich, author of _Understanding Rubrics_, defines a rubric as "_a scoring tool that lists the criteria for a piece of work, simply put, rubrics 'list what counts,' "_ based on a gradation of 1-4. Also, teachers should include exemplars for students to have a visual of what the gradations look like. I found this link, www.teach-nolgy.com, which offers several different types of rubrics.

Rubrics help students to evaluate and revise their own work. They empower students. Rubrics will also eliminate students playing "Guess What's on the Teacher's Mind", a favorite game of many teachers. No longer will you hear "I didn't know what you wanted." Or that all- time favorite "You gave me that grade because you don't like me."

The unfortunate part about a rubric is it can be time consuming for a teacher to design them. So, I would like to suggest that you design rubrics for authentic assessments and use "Criteria for Success" for all other assignments.

Criteria for Success would be number 3 on a rubric. Bottom line, for #3, the teacher will not accept anything less on an assignment but will certainly accept more. I often used this strategy, particularly for writing assignments, and I found the quality of work is amazing. Student performance was much better. In fact, by spring, the students would establish the criteria with me. In this way, everyone was invested in the assignment.

Also, using rubrics and criteria for success helps tremendously in conversations with parents. Grading/scoring becomes objective. It is based on a student's efforts on their performance. No confusion there.

Daily Assignment #49: Feedback

Feedback can be given in many forms. Primary teachers have a tendency to give feedback in the form of cute drawings, stickers and/or positive words - "Super", "Wow", "Great job", "Well done". Or at the other end of the spectrum - "You can do better", "Try again", "Try harder". Middle school and high school teachers give percentages or letter grades. There are times when all of these types of feedback are appropriate. However, none of them help students to improve their performance.

Feedback to improve student performance should be:

1. Timely
2. Specific
3. Understandable
4. Formed to allow for self-adjustment

Wiggins, 1998

I would add "in the form of a *nonjudgmental statement*" to this list.

What does nonjudgmental feedback look and sound like?
Examples:
- "This essay includes an opening sentence and 3 supporting sentences. It does not include a closing sentence." *This feedback provides the student with what they did correctly and what they need to improve on. I try not to use the word "you" in the feedback. Feedback sounds less judgmental without the word "you".*
- "The correct operation was used to solve this equation. However, the calculation is incorrect."
- "The hypothesis is stated correctly. Only two, out of the required three, forms of data have been recorded. A conclusion has not been included in this write-up."
- "This story includes a beginning, middle and ending. Punctuation marks are not included throughout the story."

If the students don't understand the feedback a rubric will provide clarity, especially if exemplars are included.

Nonjudgmental feedback takes time and a lot of thought. I suggest using nonjudgmental feedback on one set of papers the first week to practice the language and then increasing the number of sets of papers each week. The more practice the easier and quicker assessing assignments will become.

Daily Assignment #50: Best Effort

Several colleagues have asked why I close with "Best Effort." I have learned, and believe, that everything we do is based on the effort we put into it. If we and our students want to learn and be successful we must put in our best effort. Best effort includes time, practice, focus, effective strategies, resourcefulness, using feedback, and determination.

When learning something new we must use effective effort to build capacity. **Example:** In learning to ski, we must put incredible effort at the beginning. As we become better at skiing, we put in less effort because we have built capacity. For our students, learning any piece of content requires a lot of effort at the beginning, e.g. learning to read, memorizing the multiplication tables, learning the Periodic Table, Pythagorean theory, etc.

I no longer say to students "Good Luck" on a test, project, presentation, sport, etc. I always say, "Best Effort". Luck means outside influences lead to success. Luck, good or bad, applies to the lottery, and we all know how that works. Luck does not apply to learning and has no place in the classroom. "Best Effort" means success will be the result of the effort put into the test, project, etc.

I hope you will think about the language you use with your students in reference to effort and success.

In the meantime,

Best Effort!

Daily Assignment #51: Reinforcing Effort Leads to Achievement

Research shows that students may not make the connection between their level of effort and their level of achievement. As a result, teachers may need to teach this relationship. Robert Marzano states: "Students who believe the amount of effort they put into a task increases their achievement actually do better." When students meet with success when attempting to reach a specific goal, they should receive some form of recognition for their **efforts**.

Marzano's recommendations for classroom practice include:
1. Explicitly teach students that effort can improve achievement
2. Ask students to chart effort and achievement
3. Establish a rationale for recognition
4. Follow guidelines for effective and ineffective praise
5. Use recognition tokens
6. Use the pause, prompt, and praise technique (Daily Assignment #44: Pause, Prompt, Praise)

> **Classroom Instruction that Works** by Robert J.Marzano, Debra J. Pickering, Jane E. Pollock

Using rubrics helps to raise student awareness that learning is incremental and that the more effort they expend the greater their achievement will be. (Refer to Daily Assignment #48: Rubrics)

In Daily Assignment #50, I share the reasons for using the phrase "Best Effort." Changing our language as the models for our students will reinforce the importance of effort.

Daily Assignment #52: Building Capacity with Effort

When new content was introduced, whether it was learning how to read, learning borrowing or carrying, a piece of music, whatever it might have been; I would begin by putting a Popsicle stick, or anything else that can represent a bar, at the bottom of the rhombus by CAPACITY.

EFFORT

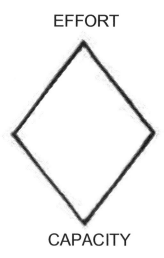

CAPACITY

I would explain that the stick was at the bottom because we were learning something new and had to put in a lot of EFFORT to build CAPACITY, which was represented by all the area above the stick.

As the students became more proficient with the material, the stick would be moved upward to represent that they had built CAPACITY, and the amount of EFFORT they needed was decreasing.

You can use this strategy with the whole class, a group, or for individuals. Keep the rhombus in a very visible place. I found the students were very encouraged and motivated by the movement of the stick.

Before you use this strategy, you will need to:

1. Name it.
2. Explain the purpose
3. Define the terms, CAPACITY and EFFORT.
4. Show how it will work.

Daily Assignment #53: Pause-Prompt-Praise

Pause- Prompt- Praise is an effective strategy for supporting students who are struggling with a particularly demanding task.

PAUSE: The student stops working on the task and talks to the teacher about the difficulty he/she is having.

PROMPT: The teacher gives the students strategies to implement.

PRAISE: When the student succeeds with the strategy/strategies praise the student for their efforts.

"Pause-Prompt-Praise." If a student is struggling, pause to discuss the problem, then prompt with specific suggestions to help her/him improve. If the student's performance improves as a result, offer praise.

> Classroom Instruction That Works: Research-Based Strategies for Increasing Student Achievement by R. Marzano, D. Pickering, & J. Pollock, ASCD, 2001

A variation of this strategy would be for the teacher to...

Pause next to the student. Sometimes just having a teacher stand nearby will trigger a connection for the student. It also sends the message that you believe in the student's ability to work on the task alone.

If the student continues to struggle...

Prompt by giving simple clues. If the student is still struggling increase the level of clues.

Examples:

1. What is the picture is of?
2. Read the start of the sentence/ end of the sentence, and let's see if we can work it out.
3. Read on a little bit more, and we will come back to it and see if we can make sense of it.
4. Looking at the picture and what is happening around this page, what do you think the word could be?

Pause between questions to give the student time to process and apply the strategy.

Praise the student's efforts in using the strategies effectively to complete the task.

Daily Assignment #54: Questions---Why do we ask the questions we ask?

We pose questions to students for many reasons. Some reasons might be:
- To determine what students know and don't know
- To develop critical and creative thinking skills
- To provide a review of material and content
- To prepare students for what is to be learned
- To engage students in discussion
- To teach students to ask questions

Sometimes we ask questions as an attention move, e.g. "Are you paying attention?" "Tim, are you with me on this?", "Maria, what are you doing?" Some questions are to check for understanding /comprehension during a lesson. A teacher might ask a question which requires a student to recall specific information. These are the "who, what, when, where, how" questions, e.g. "Who are the main characters in *To Kill A Mockingbird*?" "What is the name of the Shakespeare play about the Prince of Denmark?" "What are the names of the 5 food groups?" "When did the Cuban Missile Crisis happen?"

Here is a list of some other types of questions:
- *Rhetorical*: used for its persuasive effect without the expectation of a reply. EX: "Is the Pope Catholic?" "How much longer must women suffer this injustice?"
- *Clarification*: "Why do you say that?" "How does this relate to our conversation?"
- *Probing*: "What could we assume instead?" "What would be an example?" "What generalizations can you make?"
- *Perspectives/Viewpoints/Open Ended*: "What is another way to look at this?" "Please explain why it might be beneficial?" "What might be the strengths and weaknesses of...?"
- *Closed*: These questions require a yes or no answer. EX: "Is Athens the capital of Greece?" "Does the moon rotate around the earth?" "Did the Germans invade Norway?"

- *Hypothetical*: "What would you do if...?"
- *Reflective*: "What might you do differently next time?" "What could you have done differently?"
- *Leading*: Used to gain acceptance of your view, "You agree with me, don't you?"
- *Inference*: "What might be the reasons Ophelia went mad in *Hamlet*?"

This list is certainly not complete. There are lots of other types of questions. But this will help you to begin your thinking about why you ask the questions you ask.

Daily Assignment #55: Questions: Part 2- Designing Higher Thinking Level Questions

Questions can *"enhance student learning by developing critical thinking skills, reinforce student understanding, correct student misunderstanding, provide feedback for students, and enliven class discussions"* (Caram and Davis 2005, *Inviting Student Engagement with Questioning.* Kappa Delta Pi Record.)

Bloom identified and defined 6 question categories:

1. **Knowledge:** remember, memorize, recognize, repeat and list. These are the who, what, when, where, how questions. Examples: Who were...? What is a...? When did the...? How did...? Label...
2. **Organizing:** compare/contrast, transferring, classify, organization and selection of facts and ideas. Examples: Compare the ... Contrast the ... Classify the...
3. **Application:** problem solving, applying information, use of facts, rules and principles, show, solve. Examples: How is ... an example of...? How is ... related to...? Why is ... significant?
4. **Analysis:** subdividing, sort, categorize. Examples: What are the parts or features of...? Classify ... according to ... Outline/diagram ... How does ... Compare/contrast with...? What evidence can you list for...?
5. **Synthesis:** create, design, develop, synthesize, hypothesize, devise. Example: What would you predict/infer from...? What ideas can you add to...? How would you create/design a new...? What might happen if you combined...? What solutions would you suggest for...?
6. **Evaluation:** evaluate, development of opinions, judgments or decisions. Do you agree that...? What do you think about...? What is the most important...? Place the following in order of priority... How would you decide about...? What criteria would you use to assess...?

When planning a unit of study make sure to include higher level thinking questions, which you have designed from Bloom's 6 categories.

If you want to check the category the questions you are asking fall into, ask a colleague to observe you and write down all the questions you ask. Then sort them into management and content related. Sort the content related questions into Bloom's 6 categories.

Caram and Davis say that teachers have a tendency to "ask questions in the Knowledge category 80% to 90% of the time. These questions are not bad, but using them all the time is." Teachers need to incorporate higher order level questions into their instruction, which will require deeper thinking and more in depth responses.

> *"There are these four ways of answering questions. Which four? There are questions that should be answered categorically [straightforwardly yes, no, this, that]. There are questions that should be answered with an analytical (qualified) answer [defining or redefining the terms]. There are questions that should be answered with a counter-question. There are questions that should be put aside. These are the four ways of answering questions."* ---Buddha, Source

Daily Assignment #56: Cooperative Learning

Cooperative Learning is a phrase that is used a lot but is frequently confused with "Group Work". Cooperative Learning is different from Group Work. Group Work is random grouping of students working on an assignment or task together. Cooperative Learning begins with the teacher purposefully selecting students with various abilities to work together as a team on a project or assignment. Each team member is responsible not only for their learning but also for every other team member's learning and the completion of the task. Everyone succeeds when the group succeeds.

There is a cooperative learning structure called "Jigsaw". Students are part of a home team which consist of 4 or 5 teacher-selected students. The members of the home team break into expert groups which are made up of other students from home teams. Each expert group learns a specific assignment and then returns to their home team to teach that information. Everyone in the home teams must sign off that they know, and could represent, the home team on any of the information.

Example:

Social Justice Legends

1. The teacher divides the class into 5 groups of 4. These 5 groups are the Home Teams.

2. In each Home Team, have the students letter off---A, B, C, D.

3. As teams, all the A's are to study Martin Luther King Jr. All the B's will study Eleanor Roosevelt. The C's will study Mahatma Gandhi. And the D's will study former president Jimmy Carter. These are the expert teams. Together they go over the information on the legend and decide how they will present it to their Home Teams.

4. After a period of time, 20-30 minutes, depending on the groups and information, students return to their Home Teams to teach their legend.

5. Once each expert has completed teaching, they must be sure everyone in the Home Team understands and knows the information. Encourage Home Team members to ask clarifying questions.

6. The Home Teams number off---Home Team 1, Home Team 2, Home Team 3, Home Team 4, Home Team 5.

7. The teacher checks for understanding. The teacher draws a name of one of the legends from a hat and then a letter--- A, B, C, D, and then a Home Team number. The person with the matching letter from the Home Team drawn must give the data on the legend the teacher drew. I hope this makes sense.

There are so many benefits from doing Cooperative Learning--students working together, everyone must participate, students as teachers, efficient way to teach, students must listen and respect each other in order for learning to occur, new and interesting way to present new content, the teacher is not the teacher, to mention a few.

Here is a great link if you want more information:
http://www.jigsaw.org/overview.htm

CHAPTER 5: SCAFFOLDING LEARNING FOR STUDENTS

Daily Assignment #57: Scaffolding Learning

In the 1970s, Jerome Bruner, a cognitive psychologist, coined the phrase Scaffolding Learning, which means ways in which a learner can be supported in acquiring new knowledge, achieving a new task, or developing a new skill.

Teacher support varies, depending on the needs of the students. Support may also increase or decrease in level of intensity depending on the needs of the students.

Possible support strategies may include:

7.   Verbal or written prompts which remind students of key information.
8.   Assisting when learning a new motor skill
9.   Study guides
10. Using mnemonics to help in remembering multiple steps
11. Constructive feedback
12. Working with a partner/group
13. Using technology
14. Diagrams/graphic organizers

Example:
Teacher: What color is the sky?
Student: Blue.
Teacher: What else is blue?   Can you see something blue?
Student: I can see a blue...
The teacher in this interaction is scaffolding the student's learning about color.

Example: *Emergent Writers*
15. Teacher scribes student's words
16. Teacher and student work together
17. Student works at the writing process independently.

Example: *Teaching Graphic Organizers*
• Teacher selects G.O., fills in Main Idea and subordinate ideas, students observe.
• Teacher selects G.O., students fill in Main Idea, students and teacher fill in subordinate ideas.
• Teacher selects G.O., students fill in Main Idea and subordinate ideas
• Student selects G.O., fills in Main Idea and subordinate ideas.

In the 2nd and 3rd example the teacher gives direct instruction, prompts, specific feedback, and encouragement, and then turns the responsibility of learning over to the student until finally the teacher becomes an observer.

If possible, a teacher should try to plan in advance the type of scaffolding students will need when introducing new knowledge or skills. Scaffolding is temporary. The teacher, as in the examples above, slowly withdraws the support as the student becomes more proficient in their learning. As Vygotsky's said: "What the child is able to do in collaboration today he will be able to do independently tomorrow."

Daily Assignment #58: Building Capacity

A visual strategy I used to help my students understand how much effort it takes to build capacity was a cutout of a large rhombus. At the top of the rhombus was the word Effort. At the opposite end was the word Capacity.

EFFORT

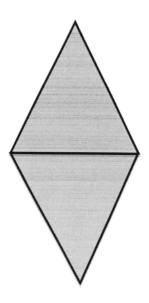

CAPACITY

When new content was introduced, whether it was learning how to read, learning borrowing or carrying, a piece of music, whatever it might have been, I would begin by putting a Popsicle stick, or anything that can represent a bar, at the bottom of the rhombus by CAPACITY. I would explain that the stick was at the bottom because we were learning something new and had to put in a lot of

EFFORT to build CAPACITY, which was represented by all the area above the stick. As the students became more proficient with the material the stick would be moved upward to represent that they had built CAPACITY and the amount of EFFORT they needed was decreasing.

You can use this strategy with the whole class, a group or for individuals. Keep the rhombus in a very visible place. I found the students were very encouraged and motivated by the movement of the stick.

Before you use this strategy, you will need to:

1. Name it.
2. Explain the purpose, including defining the terms, CAPACITY and EFFORT.
3. Demonstrate how it will work.

Daily Assignment #59: Modeling Thinking Aloud (a.k.a. MTA)

Modeling Thinking Aloud is a strategy a teacher would use to demonstrate effective strategies students might use when solving math problems, reading a difficult text, decoding a word, solving an analogy, deciding what is needed for graduation, taking a multiple choice test, or any other task. The teacher verbalizes his/her thinking as they work through a problem.

For example: Suppose during math class you'd like students to estimate the number of pencils in a school. Introduce the strategy by saying: "The strategy I am going to use today is estimation. We use it to . . . It is useful because . . . When we estimate, we . . ."

Next say: "I am going to think aloud as I estimate the number of pencils in our school. I want you to listen and jot down my ideas and actions." Then, think aloud as you perform the task.

Your think-aloud might go something like this:
"Hmmmmmm. So, let me start by estimating the number of students in the building. Let's see. There are 5 grades; first grade, second grade, third grade, fourth grade, fifth grade, plus kindergarten. So, that makes 6 grades because 5 plus 1 equals 6. And there are 2 classes at each grade level, right? So, that makes 12 classes in all because 6 times 2 is 12. Okay, now I have to figure out how many students in all. Well, how many in this class? [Counts.] Fifteen, right? Okay, I'm going to assume that 15 is the average. So, if there are 12 classes with 15 students in each class, that makes, let's see. If it were 10 classes it would be 150 because 10 times 15 is 150. Then 2 more classes would be 2 times 15, and 2 times 15 is 30. So I add 30 to 150 and get 180. So, there are about 180 students in the school. I also have to add 12 to 180 because the school has 12 teachers, and teachers use pencils, too. So, that would be 192 people with pencils." Continue in this way.

When reading aloud, you can stop from time to time and orally complete sentences like these:

      4.   So far, I've learned...
      5.   This made me think of...
      6.   That didn't make sense.
      7.   I think ___ will happen next.
      8.   I reread that part because...
      9.   I was confused by...
      10.   I think the most important part was...
      11.   That is interesting because...
      12.   I wonder why...
      13.   I just thought of...

(TeacherVision:http://www.teachervision.fen.com/skill-builder/problem-solving/48546.html?page=1)

At the end of the Think Aloud, process what you did with the students. Ask: "What were the strategies I used?" "What did they sound like?" "What did they look like?"   As the students respond, chart the strategies.   When it is time for the students to do the task on their own, refer to the strategies on the chart. Encourage the students to verbalize their thinking as they do the steps in the task.   I recommend writing a script for yourself. In this way, you will remember to include all the strategies you want the students to use. Within the script include false starts and confusions. It will be more like what the students might do when they are on their own.

Daily Assignment #60: Do Now Activities

"Do Now" activities are used at the beginning of the school day, or class, to get students engaged. They are usually a quick activity, 6-8 minutes. I recommend using a timer. It helps to keep students on task and creates an urgency to finish.

Do Now activities should be something all students can do without the teacher's assistance. They need to be engaging activities, so students want to do them and will meet with success. Consider giving extra credit for students who finish them.

Examples:
- Correct the grammar of 3 silly sentences or from familiar literature.

- Jeopardy: Give students answers and then they design the questions, e.g. Saturn, Mt. Everest, Pythagorean Theorem, tessellations.

- Trivia questions which might also be away to do a quick review before a test:
  -What presidents are still alive today? What might be 3 reasons for people to immigrate to the U.S. A.? What might be 5 reasons for global warming? What are the steps in photosynthesis and what happens in each step?

- Draw a picture: an object, symbol, explanation of an expression, homonyms, compound words

- Check it: Give 2 spelling versions of a word, math problems with some correct and incorrect answers, 2 definitions of a words - one correct- and have the students check the correct one.

- Just the Facts: a quick math facts worksheet

- Journal Writing

- Use quotes: Have students reflect and write a reaction
  - "Nothing shocks me. I'm a scientist." Harrison Ford (1942 -), as Indiana Jones
  - "Ask yourself whether you are happy and you cease to be." John Stuart Mill, English economist & philosopher (1806 - 1873)
  - quotes from Hallmark cards

Think about experimenting with this strategy one day a week and then slowly add a day.

Daily Assignment #61: 10-2

Dr. Mary Budd Rowe, a science educator, developed this 10-2 processing strategy. Simply put, 10-2 is when the teacher instructs for 10 minutes, and students have 2 minutes to process the information. Processing may include writing in a journal, reviewing and clarifying notes, sharing with a partner or with a team, and writing down questions. It is not a time to interact with the teacher, such as asking questions.

There are several advantages for doing this strategy e.g., retention of information is greater, students stay more focused during instruction, the quality of note taking and questions improves, students process with peers, independent learners are developed.

Also, I have found, when students sit for long periods of time, I lose their attention. My instruction may be amazing, but how long can anyone sit and get for an extended period of time? "The brain can absorb only what the seat will endure." I love this quotation. Unfortunately, I don't know who said it. However, it is so true. The 10-2 strategy can provide an opportunity for students to get up and move when they are sharing with a partner or a team.

I hope you will experiment with this quick and simple strategy. It doesn't cost anything, but the benefits are great.

Daily Assignment #62: Think-Pair-Share

Think-Pair-Share is a processing strategy created by Dr. Frank Lyman in 1981. There are just 3 steps to this strategy:

Step 1: Students are asked to think about a topic or a question posed by the teacher or a student.

Step 2: Students turn to a partner, or an assigned Learning Partner, (see Daily Assignment #78: Learning Partners).

Step 3: Students share or discuss their responses with partners.

Example: *Teacher*, "What data are we going to need to solve this problem?" Thinking Skill: Analyzing

Pause

Teacher, "Turn to your partner and discuss your thinking."

A variation of Step 3 might be for the students to share with their partner then create a quad with another pair and share. Another variation might be after students share with a partner, they then share with the whole class or share their partner's response.

There is also **Think-Write-Share** or **Think-Graphic Organizer-Share**. I'm sure there are many other variations as well.

Think-Pair-Share, gives students an opportunity to think, reflect, and organize their thinking. Working with a partner helps them to practice their own response and to listen to someone else's thinking.

Research shows that this strategy increases student participation, develops a higher level of thinking and questioning.

Daily Assignment #63: Paired Verbal Fluency

This is a great strategy for getting students verbally active about a topic they are about to study or are currently studying. It can, also, be a way to summarize a lesson. It also stimulates thinking and helps students recall knowledge and can be another way to use Learning Partners, (see Daily Assignment #83: Learning Partners).

It is best to give the directions one step at a time.
For example:

- "You will be working with a Learning Partner for this activity."

(Assign topic, e.g. respiratory system, reasons for the civil war, summary of homework assignment.)

- "Make eye contact with your 3:00 partner. Now go to them."

- "Decide who will be 'A' and who will be 'B'."

- "All 'A's' raise your hand. All 'B's' raise your hand."

- "When I say GO, 'A's' will talk for 60 seconds. While 'A's' are talking, 'B's' must practice good listening skills. At the end of 60 seconds I will say switch. 'B's' will talk, but cannot repeat anything."

- "'A's' have already said, and 'A's' will listen."

- "GO!" (Wait 60 seconds.)

- "SWITCH" (Wait 60 seconds.)

- "STOP"

- "During this next round we will do the same procedure, only it will be for 30 seconds each. This is your opportunity to add anything that was left out of the first round."

- "GO!" (Wait 30 seconds.)

- "SWITCH" (Wait 30 seconds.)

- "STOP"

- "This last round is for you to summarize what you heard your partner say. You will have 20 seconds each."

- "GO!" (Wait 20 seconds)

- "SWITCH" (Wait 20 seconds)

- "STOP"

- "Thank your partner and return to your seats."

When students return to their seats the teacher could do a whole class summary or have the students write their own summaries.

It is important for students to know that they are not to speak until it is their turn.

This description is of 3 rounds. Some teachers do 4 rounds, using 60, 45, 30, and 15-second intervals.

An Activator is a strategy to activate students' prior knowledge on a particular subject before a unit of study. A common Activator is the K-W-L.

K-W-L: On chart paper create 3 columns. The first column is titled, "What We Know. The second column is titled, "What We Want To Know". And the last column is titled, "What We Learned."

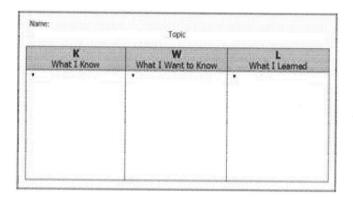

At the beginning of a unit of study, with the teacher charting, the students contribute ideas for the first two columns. All ideas should be accepted. It is not the time to discuss the ideas or the merits of whether they are right or wrong.

At the end of the unit, the third column is filled in as a way to summarize and to clarify misconceptions and misinterpretations. The students can also see the progress in their learning.

Posting the chart throughout the unit of study is a great way of reminding the students of the questions they had, and what they may have thought they knew or really did know.

For younger students, instead of "What We Know" try "What We Think We Know". Younger students believe what they know is right and as a result may state a lot of misconceptions and become

embarrassed if their statements are inaccurate. It helps to "save face" if it is stated as "What We Think We Know".
Another strategy is to put the ideas on large sticky notes. In this way, they can easily be moved from column to column.

There are many other variations of the 3 columns. Check in with colleagues to see how they use this strategy.

Daily Assignment #65: Activator-- Word Splash

For a quick review: An Activator is a strategy to activate students' prior knowledge on a particular subject before a unit of study. (*Daily Assignment #117:* Activator---K-W-L)

Let me share with you another activator called a "Word Splash". " A Word Splash is a collection of words or pictures that represent key terms or concepts from text that students are expected to learn or understand," as defined by Dr. Dorsey Hammond of Oakland University, 1985.

A Word Splash not only activates students' prior knowledge; but it also motivates students, lets students know what is important in the unit, and it actively engages students.

To create a Word Splash, the teacher selects key vocabulary/ key terms from the unit of study or a reading. In the center of a sheet of paper put the title of the unit, e.g. Islands, Civil War, Seasons, Holocaust, *To Kill A Mockingbird*, *Stuart Little*.

Then scattered around the title place the key vocabulary or terms. Students, either in partners or in a group, predict how these terms relate to the topic. All ideas must be accepted.

One student will fill the job of recorder. Set a time limit for this activity, usually 15-20 minutes, depending on the age group and the quantity of words/terms.

Example: _____

Isle	Ocean	Volcano	Continental
Peninsula	Coral Reef	Sandbar	Cove

ISLANDS

Oceanic	Islets	Desert	Australia
Inlet	Global Warming	Bay	

Don't use too many words on the Word Splash - usually 10-20, again depending on the age group. And don't use unfamiliar vocabulary. This is not a vocabulary test. Students have to know the vocabulary in order to make the predictions.

After the time limit, process the Word Splash with the whole group. As the teacher, you will quickly identify misconceptions and confusions. Another bonus of this activity is that students will be actively engaged in learning and reading about the topic because they will want to find out if their predictions were correct.

Daily Assignment #66: Activator: 5 Words-3 Words

I would like to share another Activator that I learned through Research for Better Teaching Inc. and is contained in Jon Saphier's book: _Activators_. It is a brainstorming activity titled "**5 Words-- 3Words**".

Independently, students write down 5 words that come to mind when thinking of a particular topic. Students then get into small groups, or with partners, and share their words. They decide collectively which 3 words they will share with the whole class and their reasons for selecting them.

The teacher should chart the words that each group/pair share out. Example:

Write 5 words that come to mind when you think of...

- *1776*
- *Civil Rights*
- *Ecology*
- *Weather*
- *Poetry*
- *Islands*
- *Ocean*
- *Geometry*
- *Fractions*
- *Aztecs*
- *Life Cycle*
- *Global Warming*
- *Holocaust*
- *Native Americans*
- *Family*

I have done this activity with 1st and 2nd graders, as well as older students and adults. It was very successful in activating prior knowledge.

Carousel brainstorming can be done as an activator or a summarizer. This strategy lets the teacher know what students know about a topic.

Put students in groups of 3 or 4. Each group has a sheet of chart paper and a particular color marker. On each chart paper the teacher has written a subtopic related to the main topic of study. One student serves as the recorder. Set a timer and give the students 30-45 seconds to write down on the chart paper all the terms they can think of that they associate with their subtopic.

At the end of the 30-45 seconds, the students pass their charts, keeping their assigned colored marker, clockwise to the next group. Do this until all groups have had a chance to work on all of the subtopics, and the sheets have made it around to the original groups. Each time add about 10-15 more seconds to the allotted time because it will be more challenging for students to add new information to the brainstorming list.

When the activity is completed, post the charts around the room to use for future reference. Ask the students what they noticed or what they learned from the brainstorming.

Examples:
Topic: Circulatory System

- Heart
- Lungs
- Arteries
- Veins
- Capillaries
- Gases

Topic: Database
- What is database used for?
- What do you see when viewing a database?

- What are examples of databases that we use in everyday life?
- What fields of information would you place in a database of your friends?
- What types of information do not necessarily belong in a database?

Topic: U.S. Government
- Legislative
- Executive
- Judicial
- Checks and balances

Topic: Systems of the body
- Muscular
- Skeletal
- Digestive
- Lymphatic
- Nervous
- Endocrine
- Cardiovascular

Topic: Animals
- Mammals
- Amphibians
- Reptiles
- Birds
- Insects
- Fish

Topic: Parts of speech
- Nouns
- Verbs
- Adjectives
- Adverbs
- Prepositions
- Pronouns
- Conjunctions
- Interjections

This process helps students to know that they do know something about a topic that is about to be studied. And it, also, helps students to review a topic they have just completed studying. Carousel brainstorming helps to make this connection.

Daily Assignment #68: Summarizers---3*2*1

The word 'summarize' means to give a brief statement of the main points of something. Summarizers bring closure to a lesson or a day. They are a way to assess student learning and take only 5-10 minutes. Through summarizers, teachers will discover confusions, misconceptions, or misunderstandings, and design future lessons accordingly. They can also be an effective strategy during a lesson, especially if students have been listening to a lecture or reading a lengthy piece of writing. For example, using Paired Verbal Fluency will help students to process the information before taking on more information. Summarizers help students to make connections to prior learning and to summarize their thoughts. Summarizers help students retain what they have learned. Research has shown that students who do not use a summarizer at the end of a lesson lose 85% of what they have learned within the first 24 hours.

"By teaching summarizing techniques, teachers can enhance students' ability to synthesize and organize information in a way that captures the main ideas and supporting details." Robert Marzano

3*2*1 Summarizer

Write down: **3** facts you have learned
* _____
* _____
* _____

2 facts that surprised you
* _____
* _____

1 question you have
* _____

The 3*2*1 can be adapted for the content/activity.

Other examples:
- 3 things I learned today
- 2 things I want to learn more about
- 1 question I have

- 3 ways to make $1.00
- 2 ways to make $ .50
- 1 way to make $1.00 with the fewest coins

- 3 most important things I learned
- 2 questions that still need to be answered
- 1 way this learning connects with what I learned before

- 3 important facts I've learned about photosynthesis
- 2 connections I made with other science projects
- 1 question I have after reading the text

- 3 characteristics of Scrooge
- 2 comparisons of Scrooge and Cratchit
- 1 theme of the selection

Summarizers are important strategies to include in your repertoire.

Daily Assignment #69: Summarizer--The Envelope, Please

"The Envelope, Please" is a way to get all students involved in an end of class review/summary. At the beginning of class, give each student an envelope containing a question pertaining to the lesson. At the end of the class, the teacher, randomly selects a student and asks for "The Envelope, Please." The teacher then reads the question aloud, and the student who had the envelope answers the question.

If the envelopes are sealed, you might want to give students 2 minutes before the activity to open the envelopes and work on their responses.

The questions could also be used for a written homework assignment and then used for a quick review the next day.

Daily Assignment #70: Summarizer--Ticket to Leave

Ticket to Leave is a great summarizer to use if there is only a little time left in the class or day. Students write or verbally respond to something about their learning. Responses can be written in a journal, on a slip of paper handed to the teacher as they leave the room, or said to the whole class or said to the teacher as they leave the room.

Example:

- *1 important thing you learned about…*
- *What is 1 question you have...?*
- *Solve this problem...*
- *What might be the reasons for....?*
- *What are the Main Ideas ...?*
- *Name 3 liquids.*
- *Name 3 gasses*
- *2 important things you learned on the field trip*
- *What study strategy will you use tonight to prepare for the test?*

Daily Assignment #71: Summarizer--4 Box Synectics

Synectics means bringing together diverse elements. That is what you do when using this summarizer.

The teacher draws a large box and divides it into 4 quadrants. Students name 4 everyday objects, e.g. pencil, bike, car, comb. The teacher writes one object in each quadrant. Based on the topic studied, have the students brainstorm 3-5 similes for each word.

Example:

- o How is the respiratory system like a pencil? tree? car? comb?
- o How is an atom like a...?
- o How is a quadrilateral like a...?
- o How is division like a...?
- o How is dribbling like a...?
- o How was Macbeth like a...?

This summarizer can be done as a whole group, small group, or with partners. If the students are in small groups or with partners, have students share out their favorites.

This strategy does not work with students who have not yet studied similes. They just don't understand how to make the connections. So, I recommend this strategy for grades 4-12.

Daily Assignment #72: Summarizer--The Last Word

The Last Word summarizer is actually an acronym. Students begin by brainstorming all the main ideas of a topic. Then they put them into phrases for each letter of the topic.

Examples:

M *Most frequently occurring number in a set of data*
O *Often there is more than one in large sets of numbers*
D *Data doesn't always have a mode*
E *Easy to determine; simply count how often the numbers occur*

P *Protagonist is the lead character.*
L *Lesser important adversaries may create secondary conflicts.*
A *Antagonist actively opposes the protagonist.*
Y *Yearn to express emotions and ideas appropriate to particular characters*

S *Structure of a play is broken into 5 parts.*
T *Turning point is also referred to as the climax.*
R *Rising action is complicated by secondary conflicts.*
U *Understanding the historical and cultural influences on a play*
C *Climax occurs in the third act.*
T *Tragedies end with a catastrophe.*
U *Understand the relationship of script to performance.*
R *Resolution is the moment of reversal after the climax.*
E *Exposition provides the background information.*

I have found with younger students it is best to do this as a whole class activity. At the other end of the spectrum, for older students I have found that this summarizer works best when students work with a partner or in small groups.

Daily Assignment #73: Summarizer--Get One-Give One-Move On

Get One	Give One	Move On

Get One-Give One-Move On is a strategy to help students brainstorm key ideas on a topic or reading in order to activate prior knowledge and build background knowledge. It may also be used to help students summarize and synthesize key concepts in reading.

To make a Get One-Give One-Move On:

- Set up a box matrix with six or nine boxes.

- Have students think of a question they have or an important idea about the topic or reading and write it in the first box.

- Set up a rotation pattern – ex. pass to the left - by telling students to pass the sheet to another student. Another way might be to have students get up and find someone to exchange papers with.

- Students read what was written in the first box and write an idea in box 2. No ideas can be repeated on a paper. If their idea already appears on the paper, the student has to think of another idea to write.

- Students continue passing on each paper or exchanging papers, reading the ideas, and adding new ideas until all the boxes are filled with ideas.

Each sheet is returned to the original owner to read and reflect upon.

To take this strategy to the next level have students write a summary using the ideas on their paper.

Possible Topics:

        Writing topics
        Possible reasons for the Civil War
        Possible reasons for the Civil Rights Movement
        Geometric shapes
        Classroom rules/expectations
        Healthy snacks
        Rules for basketball
        Woodwind instruments
        Words with 4 syllables
        Reptiles
        Warm-blooded animals

The Get One – Give One strategy does take some prep time, and it can be tough to teach students the procedure the first few times around. However, it's well worth it because it gets students to engage in academic conversation in a low-risk environment. By the time it's time for a class discussion, each student has already practiced sharing an idea with a few peers. It keeps every student accountable and is a great way to increase the energy of the class!

Also, this is a wonderful exercise to do with colleagues. It is a great way to share strategies for classroom management, teaching a content area, etc. Try it at a staff or team meeting. You'll be surprise at what your colleagues know.

Daily Assignment #74: Summarizer--Inside-Outside Circle

Inside-Outside Circle is a summarizing strategy developed by Spencer Kagan. This is a great strategy to get students to interact with each other and to get them up and moving. It is especially helpful for ESL students who need to practice oral language.

Procedure:

1. Half of the students stand up and form an inner circle, facing out. They are Partner A.
2. The other half of the class forms an outer circle – each one facing a partner from the inside circle. They are Partner B.
3. Put a question or a statement on a board, or have students summarize a text, etc...
4. Give the students "Think Time", about 10-15 seconds.
5. Partner A shares their response for 1 minute.
6. Partner B shares their response for 1 minute.
7. Ring a bell or chime or just say "Switch".
8. The outside circle slides 2 people to the left or right.
9. Repeat #5,6,7, 8 alternating which Partner responds first.

The teacher needs to decide how many times the circle moves and how long the responses should be. Some teachers shorten the response time each time the circle moves.

This is also a good strategy for the teacher to do an assessment of student learning. The teacher stands in the middle of the inner circle and listens to the conversations.

Daily Assignment #75: Summarizer--Numbered Heads Together

The structure of Numbered Heads is from the work of Spencer Kagan. There are a number of variations on this strategy. Some are very simple, and others have a greater degree of complexity.

The purpose of Numbered Heads is to process information, communication, developing thinking, review of materials, and check prior knowledge.

This strategy can be used as a precursor to teaching Cooperative Learning structures, such as a Jigsaw.

STEPS:

- Divide the class into equal groups of 4. Number off the students in each group. If one group is smaller than the others have #3 answer for #4 as well. The teacher can give numbers or students can give numbers themselves.

- Teacher asks the students a question or sets a problem to solve. It must be stressed that everyone in the group must be able to participate and answer the question.

- Ensure enough time is given for the group to do the task.

- The students work together. They quite literally "put their heads together" in order to solve the problem and also ensure that everyone in the group can answer the question.

- The teacher asks for an answer/response to a question by calling a number. This might be random, e.g. pulling a number out of a hat, or can initially be decided by the teacher in order to ensure the process is successful)

- The students with the number called then answers/responds to the question.

This is a great strategy for students to learn how to work together and to be responsible for each other's learning.

Another processing strategy is 37-90. The theory behind the 37-90 strategy, is for every 37 minutes of instruction, students need to get up, (and I stress get up), and process the information. It is that simple. However, as simple as it is, it will have a tremendous impact on student learning.

This strategy would be more effective for older students. Younger students would have difficulty sitting for 37 minutes. Now that I think about it, I know of adults who would have difficulty sitting for 37 minutes, including myself.

I know of middle and high school teachers who have used this strategy - particularly if they have 90 minute block classes. One high school teacher reported, "This was good for all the students in the class. I don't like a lot of moving around in the classroom. However, after using this strategy only once, the students seemed less drowsy, and a slightly happier tone developed in the class."

So, when planning a lesson make sure to include processing time.

CHAPTER 6: EFFECTIVE STRATEGIES FOR TEACHERS

Daily Assignment #77: Charting

While everyone seems to be using high tech in teaching, I think flip charts are still a very effective tool.

Here are some tips for preparing charts:

COLORS: For colors use the most comfortable for people to focus on. Use earth colors, instead of black for the text, e.g. blue for the sky, green for the ground and brown for the earth, yellow for highlighting and red ONLY for critical emphasis. Avoid using the colors purple, pink, or orange. They are extremely difficult to see. And avoid using too many colors. Using one dark color and one accent color works best. Use color for impact - not to be artsy.

LETTERING: Lettering should be at least 2" high. Titles should be in CAPS. Use upper and lower case letters in text. Write clearly. Print, as cursive is difficult to read at a distance.

VISUAL GRAPHICS: Use bullets in front of phrases. Box in parts of text. Draw lines between key lines.

BANNERS: Put the topic in a banner at the top of the chart. Outline it in black and read and fill in background with yellow.

- You can write lightly in pencil any notes next to key points you need. The students won't be able to see them.

- If you make any mistakes, you can use "whiteout" or a slip of paper to correct any small errors.

- For larger areas, cover the mistake with a double layer of flip chart paper and correct the error.

- Making "prepared" flip charts can take a considerable amount of time. Make sure you start preparing your charts early enough so you can review them and make any changes or corrections beforehand.

- It takes practice to learn how to print neatly. If you do not have neat printing, ask someone who does to prepare the charts for you. A poorly prepared flip chart can be very distracting.

Daily Assignment #78: Calling Sticks

Sometimes teachers have a tendency to call on the same students to answer our questions, or to do certain jobs, or for lots of other reasons, and we don't even realize it. However, the students know. Some students know you'll never call on them, so they just stop listening.

Calling sticks will help teachers to make sure to give everyone an opportunity. It is such a simple strategy and very effective.

Write each student's name on a Popsicle stick. Place them in a can or cup.

At your next Q&A session, ask the question first, and then draw a name. Don't draw the name first. If the name is drawn first, the rest of the class stops listening.
After the student responds put the stick back in the can. This lets the student know that they may be called on again, so they need to pay attention. If the teacher puts the stick aside, the student will tune the teacher out because they will think the teacher is done with them.

Calling sticks are a great way to assign classroom jobs. Just randomly pick a name out of the can. I also used them to choose who would read a passage from a book; who would share their math strategies; who would go first, second, third... for dismissal or lining up; and for assigning partners. You will discover that you will use them throughout the day for many things.

You will also find that the onus is not on the teacher anymore. The students can no longer say, "You always call on _____."

Teachers who have more than one class have a set of sticks for each group, or assign numbers to students and have numbers on the sticks instead of names. Another approach might be to number the desk instead of assigning numbers to the students. High School teachers have used this approach.

I know you will see a difference in students' attention and participation when using this strategy.

Daily Assignment #79: Dipsticking

Madeline Hunter, an education theorist, is credited for coining this term. Dipsticking, as a teaching strategy, is a metaphor for checking for understanding. Car engines contain a dipstick to check the oil supply. It is used to determine if more oil needs to be added to the car. Dipsticking in teaching does the same thing, and it takes very little time. Dipsticking is used frequently throughout instruction to check on students' understanding and to see if more instruction is needed before moving on. If the students consistently answer the questions correctly, then the teacher can assume that the lesson is going well.

There are two types of Dipsticking

1. Student self-evaluation
2. Direct content checks.

Examples of quick <u>student self-evaluations</u> are:

- Ask your students to nod their heads if they're with you
- Ask for a thumbs-up or thumbs-down signal to indicate how well they understand a concept that has just been presented.

However, the one significant problem with self- evaluation is that the students may think they understand the content material when they actually don't.

Hence, <u>direct content checks,</u> that quickly evaluate recall and comprehension of the material presented, may provide the clearest answers for the teacher.

Example:

- Create a brief oral true/false quiz and have the whole class respond with a thumbs-up or thumbs-down signal.

Remember, the entire class must be answering the question for you to be able to make a correct visual assessment of their understanding. Too many teachers rely on a correct answer from a single student and assume that the rest of the class gets it.

Whenever you reach a benchmark in your instruction, or a certain point where the entire class should understand a piece of content, or their eyes glass over and the fog has settled in, dipstick!! You'll give yourself the opportunity to correct misunderstandings and keep your students with you consistently throughout the lesson.

Daily Assignment #80: Chunking Instruction Within a Lesson

Chunking Instruction is when a teacher varies the activities within a lesson to keep a quick pace and to address different learning styles.

The lesson structure might look like this:

1. Teacher does direct instruction: Teacher explains how the Greeks explained things in nature and gives an example.

2. Small group interaction: Groups of 3 students spend about 5 minutes thinking about other myths that explain elements in nature.

3. Whole group sharing: Groups report out on their thinking.

4. Small groups apply skills/knowledge: The small groups now write their own original myth explaining an element of nature.

5. Whole group sharing: Groups share their stories.

6. Teacher does direct instruction: Explains characteristics of several Greek Heroes.

7. Small group interaction: Groups select a hero and, using a descriptive graphic organizer, list the characteristics.

8. Whole group sharing: Groups share their graphic organizers.

9. Individual students apply knowledge/skills independently: Each student must create a myth which explains an element of nature and include at least 1 Greek Hero.

By doing a lesson this way, you are addressing the introverted and extroverted learners in your class among other learning styles. The pace is quick, which helps with attention. The students have an opportunity to take in learning, discuss it, and apply it many times in different ways. Because students have had opportunities to practice within small groups before they work independently, the success of the writing assignment will be greater.

I hope this helps with your thinking while designing your lesson plans. It **will** make a difference in students' learning.

Daily Assignment #81: Predicting What Can Go Wrong

We can never predict everything that can go wrong within a lesson, herding students, or any other situation within a school day. However, we can try to be mindful of possibilities e.g., challenging vocabulary within a lesson, confusing directions for an activity, obstacles blocking a passageway, students upset over a change in the schedule, conflicts on the playground, and the list goes on.

How can we prevent these situations? As you plan the day, take a moment and think what might interfere with a smooth flow within a lesson, transitions, recess, rescheduling, etc. Then try to plan for it. For example, look at the vocabulary within a lesson, list challenging words, teach the meaning, clarify questions, then do the lesson. For some lessons, it is hard to know what can go wrong until you've taught it. Then it may become crystal clear as to what to anticipate the next time.

When giving directions for an activity; ask the students for thumbs up if they understand, thumbs sideways if they have one question and thumbs down if they are totally confused. Then clarify the misunderstandings and/or confusions.

When herding students be mindful of obstacles e.g., other classes moving in the hallways; equipment - video carts, wastebaskets, furniture, etc. - in awkward places; puddles of water or, dare I say, even bodily fluids. Don't be unnerved if you must take a different route and have to move things around to create that passageway.

Plan for it if you know that some students may have a difficult time during recess. Hold them back and have a conversation with them about appropriate behavior during recess. In this way, you are giving them notice and being very clear about expectations.

In our profession, change in the daily schedule is inevitable. There are so many unpredictable events that can impact our day e.g., an unplanned assembly, fire drills, conflict among students, specialist absences, announcements on intercom, someone getting hurt emotionally/physically, etc. All of these impact instruction. How you handle these events will be a model for your students. Remain calm and flexible. Have back up plans that you keep on hand. Refer to Daily Assignment #26 for ideas to fill those down moments that may result from a schedule change.

Of course, you can't predict everything. Learn from each event. Build your repertoire and be calm.

Daily Assignment #82: Forming Groups

It can be a challenge to form groups quickly for various activities.   If students are asked to do it on their own, they, of course, have a tendency to select their friends, of course. Also, there are children who are never picked for various reasons.

If the teacher selects the groups, the students will blame the teacher if they are in a group they are not happy with. Using the strategies listed below will help to eliminate the blame problem because it is luck of the draw. It has nothing to do with the teacher.

Strategies for forming random groups quickly:

*Numbered Heads--students count off 1-5. All the ones work together, all the twos, and so on. Or 1,2,3,4,5 makes a group and so on.

*Using a deck of cards have all the aces form a group, kings another, and so forth.

*Use different colored pieces of paper have all the red pieces form a group, greens another, blues a third, etc.

*Plastic animals. There are so many different types you can purchase. Lions form a group, elephants another group, etc.

*Different colored counting bears, unifix cubes, pattern blocks, M&M's (a favorite). All these and many others lend themselves to forming groups.

For pairing students up quickly, these strategies work as well. Using "Old Maid" cards works. And try to find an "Old Bachelor" deck of cards.

All of these strategies work for students, K-12. High School students get a kick out of getting plastic animals, counting bears, etc., as much as the younger students do.   The challenge will be getting them all back.

Daily Assignment #83: Learning Partners

I would like to share with you a strategy for establishing Learning Partners in the classroom.

1. Make a large analog clock on an 8-1/2 by 11 sheet of paper with only the hours - no hands or minute lines. Draw a line extending into the center from each hour. At the top of the page have a space for the students to write their name.

2. Have a quick, snappy piece of music to play during this activity.

3. Hand out the sheets of paper and have them write their name at the top. Do not explain the purpose of the exercise. Otherwise they will get only their friends to sign their clock.

4. Explain that once the music starts, they are to get up and exchange papers with 12 other people. Example: I would give my clock to Tim, he would put his name at 1:00, and I would put my name at 1:00 on his clock. Then I would find someone else and have that person sign another hour, and I would need to sign the same hour on their clock. If they already have someone for that hour, I would need to skip them and go to someone else. I highly recommend that you model this for your students. If the directions are not clear, you will end up with a huge mess. I sure hope what I've written is clear for you.

5. After a few students have finished, stop the music and have everyone sit down.

6. You will need to go over the clock and ask who does not have a partner for each hour. This is very time consuming, but the benefits are worth it. You then start pairing up the remaining students. If you have an extra student, they become the substitute or you can create triads. Example: Teacher, " Who does not have a 2:00 partner?" Three students raise their hands. "Okay, Jane, you put Regina down for 2:00. And Regina, you put down Jane for 2:00."

7. Collect the papers and then explain to the students what the purpose of the clocks will be.

8. Make copies for yourself. Older students have a tendency to change them or lose them. Have them keep a copy in their notebook or some place they can refer to them quickly. If you are a self- contained classroom, post them for quick reference.

Helpful Hints:
   * When you use Learning Partners always give the directions for the activity before you assign the Learning Partner. If you say which Learning Partner it is first, the students will focus on that person and not the directions for the activity.

   * Whenever you want to pair students together you should say, "Make eye contact with your 3:00 partner. Go to them. That is who you will be working with today." Making eye contact first helps them to go to that person. Otherwise, they may not get there.

   * Make a note to yourself that you used the 3:00 partner so you won't use it the next time. You'll never remember on your own, trust me. It will also eliminate the students complaining about always having to work with the same person.

   * You do not have to use a clock pattern for setting up partners. You can use content-related designs. For example, I used geometric shapes-- rhombus, trapezoid and hexagon. I would say, " Make eye contact with your rhombus partner." In this way, I was teaching the shapes, as well as pairing students.
Some teachers have used U.S. states--"Make eye contact with your Florida partner." Another one might be continents, parts of a plant, water cycle, famous artist, or musicians. The list is endless.

Daily Assignment #84: Posting the Agenda

Have you ever attended a professional development workshop and wondered where is this instructor going with this lesson, or what is going to happen next, or what are we going to do with this information, or when is the break? Well, you have students in your class asking the same questions.

Posting the agenda will answer your students' questions. The students will know what they will be doing with the information, what each step will be to get there, and when it will end.

Also, posting the agenda helps the students – and the teacher – to be more focused and to stay on task.

The agenda can be posted for an entire day or for a lesson. When posting the agenda for the day, some teachers put the times beside each event.

Example of an all-day agenda:

8:25 Morning Meeting
8:45 Literacy
10:00 Working Snack
10:30 Recess
11:00 Lunch
11:30 Math
12:15 Science
12:45 Music
1:15 Social Studies
2:00 Clean-up
2:10 Closing Meeting
2:25 Dismissal

Lesson: Parallelograms (Daily Assignment #46: Concept Attainment)
1. Using a T chart, examples of parallelograms and non- parallelograms
2. Learning Partners create a definition
3. More examples

4. Partners edit definition
5. More examples
6. Final edit of definition
7. Using partner definitions, group creates a definition
8. Final definition
9. Parallelogram designs

This lesson was taught to a group of second graders.

Daily Assignment #85: Interruptions During Instruction

We all have them - interruptions during Instruction, unwelcome intrusions, e.g. intercom announcements, custodian collecting trash, a student entering the classroom late, parents who drop by, colleagues who want to borrow something, and the list goes on. A day can seem like a series of interruptions with some instruction happening in between.

So, how do we handle these interruptions? Some teachers allow them and then just continue instruction where they left off before the interruption. Other teachers do not allow them. They might turn off the intercom speaker, or put the trash barrels outside the classroom door so the custodian doesn't come into the class, or put a do not disturb sign on the door. I've known upper grade teachers who have locked their classroom door so that students who are late do not come in and interrupt instruction. And then there are teachers who totally ignore the intrusion and press on.

 I think most teachers match their response to the intrusion. A response to a student interruption may be very different than a response to a colleague interrupting instruction. The response might also depend on the type of interruption, e.g. the teacher is teaching a concept to a small group of students and a student from another group comes over to ask a question versus the teacher is teaching a concept to a small group of students and a student shouts out a question from across the room.

Whatever the response to the interruption, it sends a message to the students as to what is important to you.

CHAPTER 7: EFFECTIVE LEARNING STRATEGIES TO TEACH STUDENTS

Daily Assignment #86: Graphic Organizers

Graphic organizers are visual tools which represent thinking skills. There are many different kinds, depending on the thinking skill. I would like to share 3 of my favorites.

The Descriptive Graphic Organizer is used for identifying characteristics. This is a commonly used one. Another name for this graphic organizer is the Web or Wheel. When using the Descriptive Graphic Organizer, not only have the students put a characteristic on the lines coming out from the center circle, but at the end of the line draw a box and put evidence to support the characteristic. For example: A characteristic of the big bad wolf in The Three Little Pigs is that he is persistent. The evidence is that he continued to chase the little pigs after failing several times.

Students have a great deal of difficulty summarizing. They have a tendency to copy the book or information. The Sequential Graphic Organizer is a great visual tool for summarizing an article, book, event, or steps in directions. It is a series of connecting linear boxes. For example, K-1 students may just have 3 boxes. Second graders may have 5 boxes. Older students can make decisions on how many boxes they would need, keeping in mind that a summary is an abbreviated version of the original information.

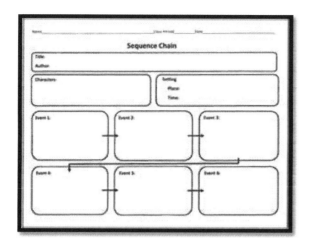

The third graphic organizer is the Compare and Contrast, a.k.a. Venn Diagram. I prefer the Double Bubble design to the Venn Diagram. I can never fit in all the information in the oval center shape. The Double Bubble has 2 rectangles with lines coming out on one side of each rectangle, connecting to squares. Between the 2 rectangles, in the center of the paper, there is another column of circles, with connecting lines to both rectangles. The 2 things being compared would be in the rectangles. The things that are different would be in the outside squares and those that are similar or the same in the center circles.

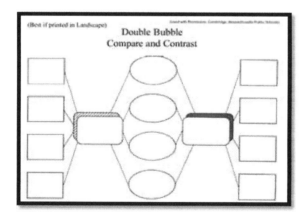

Daily Assignment #87: Introducing a Descriptive Graphic Organizer

In Daily Assignment #5: Community Building Activity, I described the Artifact Bag, (a.k.a. "All About Me Bag") and how to implement the activity. This Daily Assignment is how to take it up a notch by adding a visual tool to represent a higher level thinking skill--Recognizing Attributes or, perhaps, Identifying Characteristics and Deductive Thinking.
That was a mouthful.

Before you present this activity to your students, make sure you:
1. Tell them you will be using a descriptive organizer
2. Describe its purpose
3. Show them how it will be used

For each student you should prepare an 8 1/2 x 11 heavy piece of paper by drawing a circle in the center about 3 inches in diameter, then draw 4-5 lines coming out from the circumference line. At the end of each line draw a small rectangle or circle.

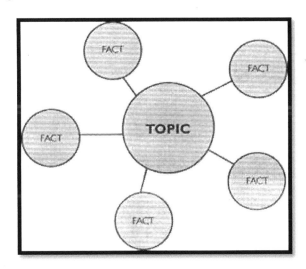

As you share an Artifact Bag write on the rectangle/circle what the object is and on the lines write the students' guesses as to what that object tells them about the person. If the students guess who the person is, write the person's name in the center circle. If they don't guess correctly, put the objects back in the bag and put the graphic organizer aside for another time. Also, somewhere on the paper add their photos once they have been guessed.

You have just introduced the Descriptive Graphic Organizer, and modeled it for the class, 20-30 times with each Artifact Bag. Depending on the age group, the students may be able to do this activity after the teacher has modeled the steps 10-15 times. Think of all the wonderful skills you have introduced by doing this activity, e.g. community building, higher level thinking skills, and possibly leadership roles.

Now, you have a great beginning of the year bulletin board. As students are guessed, put their self- portraits (see Daily Assignment #4: Plans for the 1st Day), descriptive graphic organizer and photo together on display. Everyone loves to see the comparison of the self-portrait and photo, plus they get to learn a little something about your students/class.

Daily Assignment #88: Teaching Graphic Organizers

Teachers have a tendency to give students graphic organizers and assume that students know how to use them. Each type of graphic organizer needs to have a specific lesson which explains its purpose and use.

In the first lesson, the teacher needs to choose and model the graphic organizer and – along with students – fill in the pertinent data. The next time a graphic organizer is used, the teacher fills in the main topics and information with the students. The next time, the students fill in the main topics and with the teacher they fill in the information. The next time, the students fill in the main topics and the information independently. Letting students take responsibility for the graphic organizer in steps ensures more success when they are required to complete one independently.

Notice I keep saying "the next time." That's because it may be necessary for the teacher to model a particular step many times before students are able to do the work independently.

Use the same graphic organizer many times and in different content areas. Thinking skills and graphic organizers, as a rule, are not content specific. Students need to recognize this as well.

Also, when introducing a graphic organizer, I recommend using familiar content so that the focus is on how to use the graphic organizer, not on new content.

Daily Assignment #89: Cornell Note-Taking

How many of you have heard these comments when students have not been able to take notes during a lecture, reading text, or watching a video?
- "I can't write down everything the teacher says because the teacher talks too fast."
- "The notes that I take are not organized."
- "I can't understand what I have written."
- "My notes don't help me when I study."
- "I can't focus on note-taking because I get distracted."

The Cornell Note-Taking method provides a systematic format for condensing and organizing notes. Walter Pauk, a professor of education at Cornell University, created Cornell Note-Taking.

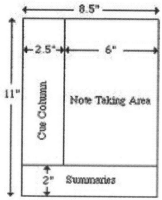

The student divides the paper into 1/3 and 2/3 column. The 2/3 column, on the right, is for taking detailed notes. Note: Students should avoid using long sentences. To help with quick note-taking students need to be taught symbols and abbreviations. The 1/3 column, on the left, is the Key Ideas column. The bottom of the page has a horizontal line across, about 2 inches from the bottom, for a summary.

The opposite page - on the left side of the notebook - should be divided using a horizontal line ¼ of the page from the bottom. In the 3/4 section, students rewrite the information in a different format; such as in a graphic organizer, drawing, graph, etc. In the bottom 1/4, students design relevant questions.

Now, when it is time to study for a test, the student has a concise, detailed, readable set of notes. The student can cover up the note-taking column to answer the questions that they designed or to identify the Key Ideas.

Let's take a count of how many times and ways a student visits the information:
1. Hears or sees the information and
2. Takes notes
3. Revisits notes to identify Key Ideas
4. Writes a summary
5. Reconfigures the information into a graphic organizer, a drawing,   etc.

And finally...
6. Designs relevant questions

After seeing the information 6 times the likelihood of students recalling the information is very high because they are actually doing something with the information. The recall is much higher than if the students just take notes.

When teaching this strategy, as with all other strategies, use familiar content so the students focus on the structure not the content.

Here is a link I discovered for designing Cornell Note-taking paper:
http://incompetech.com/graphpaper/cornelllined

It would be a great strategy to begin teaching the first week of school and then use throughout the year. Even better would be for a team of teachers to agree that this will be the main study skill taught and used by all teachers for the year.
Go for it!!!

Daily Assignment #90: Memory Joggers--Mnemonics-Acronyms

Mnemonics are devices, such as patterns of letters, ideas, associations, that assist in remembering something.

A mnemonic for remembering lists consists of an easily remembered acronym or phrase with an acronym that is associated with the list items. For example, to remember the colors of the rainbow use the mnemonic: Richard Of York Gave Battle In Vain or ROY G BIV.

Here's a list of other acronyms:
- Planets: My Very Excellent Mother Just Made Us Nine Pizzas.

- Points on a compass: Never Eat Sour Watermelons: points on compass

- First 20 Periodic Table Elements: Hi! He Lies Because Boran Can Not Oxide Fluoride. New Nation Might Sign Peace Security Clause. A King Can.

- Great Lakes: HOMES

Spelling mnemonics are all about creating a verse or phrase to help remember how to spell the more difficult words. Often the sillier they are the easier they are to remember.

These mnemonics have come from many different sources.
- PIEce of PIE
- You hEAR with your EAR.
- There is a LIE in believe.
- Is it a son or sun? - A son is a boy and they both have an o.
- A friEND is always there when the END comes.
- I before E except after C - and when saying "A" as in neighbor or weigh, and weird is just weird
- Always smell A RAT when you spell separate.
- When 2 vowels go walking the first does the talking.

- The silent e makes the vowel say its name. e.g. mat/mate
- When you eat deSSert you always come back for the seconds.
- Your principal is your PAL - the difference between principal and principle
- "TO GET HER" - remember how to spell together because if you "get her", you'll be together.
- When you assume you make an ass out of u and me
- Your SECRETary will keep your SECRET
- BR! Its FeBRuary in New England
- Practice/Practise - ICE is a noun so practICE is a noun and practise is a verb - Soccer practice improves your game, so you need to practise regularly.
- Meat/meet - I like to eat meat
- An island is land
- Where, here, there, everywhere - Place names all have here in them
- Stationary/stationery - Stationery contains *er* and so does paper; stationary (not moving) contains *ar* and so does car
- Loose/Lose - Loops are loose and it is easy to lose a shoe.
- Wherever there is a Q there is a U.
- Affect is the action
- Effect is the result or end.
- Complement/Compliment - Complement adds something to make it enough and a compliment puts you in the limelight.
- Special - The CIA have special agents.

Next time a student has a problem with a more difficult spelling word consider creating a mnemonic. If a student is having difficulty remembering a list of things, create an acronym to help them remember.

Daily Assignment #91: Number Scrolls

I would like to describe a math strategy called "Scrolls". Scrolls are amazing math tool for grades 1-3. I do believe, though, that having students begin a scroll in first or second grade continuing to work on the scrolls in the upper grades should be considered. I've had students start a scroll in first grade and continue to do it in 3rd, 4th and 5th grade. If you decide to start scrolls in the upper grades, of course, begin with much higher numbers, such as in the 10,000's. However, you'll be surprised how many of your students need practice with lower numbers.

The advantages of using scrolls are that they provide a deeper understanding of numbers, recognition of number patterns, and clarity with place value. They also provide practice in writing numbers, which students need a lot of.

You will need a paper towel roll and 10x10, 1 inch graph paper. Tape a piece of graph paper to the roll. Write the students name on the inside of the roll. Believe me when I say that this is necessary. It will prevent unrolling the scrolls to find a name.

Fill in the graph as I have done below. Putting in negative integers teaches students that there are numbers below zero as well as above zero. It is also showing the students the directions of the numbers.

Let the students finish the page. They will get to 80. Line up and tape on the next sheet. The students continue counting up and you keep adding paper. I've had a student get up to 12,000 on his scroll.

You should check every 2 rows when the students first begin writing on their scrolls. This will help to prevent mistakes and possibly causing a big mess.

L	I	N	D	A					
-9	-8	-7	-6	-5	-4	-3	-2	-1	0
1	2	3	4	5	6	7			

Scrolls are a phenomenal strategy. I swear by them. I used them all the time in my classroom. I believe scrolls should be a requirement K-3. The students loved them. Some students struggled with them at the beginning. Some students became very competitive with them, which I squashed because I didn't want them used that way. Scrolls really helped the students who did number reversals and transposing.

CHAPTER 8: MESSAGES TEACHERS SEND AND RECEIVE

Daily Assignment #92: The Pygmalion Effect

Often teachers have an expectation and a belief as to how students will perform or behave. It is called the Pygmalion effect. It is named after a Cypriot sculptor from Greek mythology who fell in love with a female statue he had carved out of ivory. The effect is also known as the Rosenthal effect, after psychologist Robert Rosenthal who studied this phenomenon and published a report on it in 1968.

The Pygmalion effect is a form of self-fulfilling belief or perception by a teacher, whether negative or positive, which impacts student performance.

In his study Rosenthal predicted that when given information that certain students had higher IQs than others, teachers might unconsciously behave in ways that facilitate and encourage the students' success and the inverse happening for students with lower IQs.

In the study, a number of teachers were informed that certain students in their class had scored higher on academic and intelligence tests. The teachers were asked to track the progress of those students through the school year. Not surprisingly, those students performed at higher academic levels.

There was one snag in the experiment: The students that Rosenthal had said were academically gifted actually weren't any different from the rest of the students in the class.

James Rhem, executive editor for the online National Teaching and Learning Forum, commented: "When teachers expect students to do well and show intellectual growth, they do; when teachers do not have such expectations, performance and growth are not so encouraged and may in fact be discouraged in a variety of ways."

Teachers send expectations and their beliefs about student learning through their words, actions, lessons/assignments, body language, attitude and responses to students' answers and questions. Teachers must be vigilant in all these areas and in some I haven't even mentioned.

Daily Assignment #93: Messages Teachers Send Through Body Language

Our body language and expressions convey to students how we think or feel about what they are saying or doing. Body language/nonverbal communication includes: facial expressions, eye contact, body movement, spatial distance, and posture. Sometimes we are not even aware of our body language and the messages we are sending to students.   Through facial expressions a teacher can communicate enthusiasm, warmth, assertiveness, confidence, expectations, feelings, or displeasure. Just the slightest movement of an eyebrow sends a message to the students. Using eye contact, or not, when a student is speaking sends another message. It can mean I'm either interested in what you have to say or I'm not interested. Direct eye contact can also communicate disapproval.   I mastered "The Look" and used it a lot for classroom management. As one student described it, "Linda does a scary look." No words are necessary.

Teachers communicate through how they stand and where, also in where they sit, e.g. on a desk, chair or stool, in walking around the room, in use of arms, e.g. folding arms, throwing them up in the air, pointing, in leaning toward or away from students, in hands on hips, etc.

When a student is speaking, leaning head or body forward sends the message that you are listening and interested. When smiling frequently the message communicated is one of friendliness. Maintaining eye contact sends the message that you are interested. Crossed arms communicate an unwillingness to engage or defensiveness, while uncrossed arms communicate openness. Becoming fidgety indicates a loss of interest. So, leave that stack of papers alone while a student is talking. Whatever you do, don't clench your fists. That message is very clear and scary. Frowning shows disapproval, and that's okay. Just don't do it all day, or you'll get frown lines.

http://www.stanford.edu/group/SLIP/TIPS/Teaching.html

Teachers can use all of these behaviors as nonverbal behavioral management strategies.

Bottom line, teachers need to become much more aware of their body language so that they promote student learning and not shut it down.

Consider having a peer observe and collect data on your body language in 30-45 minute blocks of time. The data will enable you to recognize the behaviors that you may need to foster or to completely eliminate.

Daily Assignment #94: Messages Teachers Send When Responding To Students

Teachers send many messages when responding to students' comments, questions/answers, etc. Unconsicously, and sometimes consciously, we send positive and negative messages through our responses whether verbal or non-verbal.

It is difficult to always manage our responses. Sometimes we don't even realize that we just gave a sigh or rolled our eyes to a student's comment or answer. Imagine how that student feels hearing or seeing the teacher respond in that way. We might be giving certain students positive responses such as, "That's right, very good" or something even simpler as a smile with a nod. Then we just nod or give some other subtle response to the next student. The 2nd student is now wondering what they said that was wrong, and why the teacher didn't like their response. The rest of the class is thinking the first student is the smart one. Also, they are afraid they may not give a response the teacher will like next time.

Of course, there are much more extreme examples of teachers' responses and the impacts they have on students. There are teachers who will berate students for giving an incorrect response or an awkward comment. Guess what message they're sending?

This is not to say that a teacher shouldn't address a wrong answer. But it should be done in a respectful way. I know of a teacher who would make a buzzer sound if the answer was wrong, and of another who would shout "WRONG". How humiliating for a student!

If a student gives an incorrect response or says something that doesn't make sense, stick with them. Help them save face. You might want to ask follow-up questions for clarification. A teacher's response can either spur learning forward or shut it down.

Consider having a colleague come in to observe your teaching. Have them collect data on your responses to students. It's a great way to learn what kind of messages you are sending your students.

Daily Assignment #95: Teacher Talk

Teachers need to be more cognizant of how much talking they do in the class and try to restrict their talking to vital moments during instruction. Research shows that teachers talk *70-80%* of the time during a typical lesson and students speak for *20-30%* of the time. No wonder we are exhausted. It should be the other way around with teachers speaking *20-30%* of the time.

There are lessons that require more direct instruction/ teacher talk. However, keep in mind the average learner's attention span is 10-18 minutes. If you are teaching a 45-minute class and are talking from the beginning to the end, just know that your students have shut you off after the first 10-15 minutes. So, plan well.

If teachers talk only during vital moments of instruction, the students are more likely to listen because they know that when the teacher talks it must be important.

Also, teachers need to be aware of the language and vocabulary they use, therefore modeling for students. Students need to talk more in class, of course, on topic. In this way, students have more opportunities to use language and vocabulary related to the topic and to demonstrate their skills. The teacher will also have another form of assessment.

Daily Assignment #96: Adjusting Speech

Have you ever noticed that you have a different speech pattern when you speak with friends or family or parents of your students than when you are teaching or speaking to your students?   We are adjusting our speech all day long to match the people and the situations.

We need to model and teach adjusting of speech for our students so that they recognize their speech patterns and what appropriate speech in the classroom sounds like.

Students need to be taught how to differentiate between how they speak to their friends and how they should speak in a learning environment.

We need to provide opportunities for students to not only hear the difference but to also see it in writing as well. All the time model what is appropriate speech in the classroom.

In the meantime, become more cognizant of how you speak in different situations. My family has pointed out to me many times when I am using my "teacher speech" with them.

Daily Assignment #97: Listening Skills

In Daily Assignment #90 I wrote about "Teacher Talk". In this Daily Assignment I am focusing on the listeners- the students. Research has shown that we remember 25-50% of what we hear. That means if you are doing direct instruction for 10 minutes, students pay attention to less than half of your instruction. This also applies to when teachers are giving directions. Bottom line: Teachers need to make sure that they say the important stuff up front and talk less throughout the lesson. The students aren't listening anyway.

We need to teach students to be better listeners. The research I have read on this topic indicates that the most important strategy for teaching students listening skills, is modeling by the teacher. In the book, *In the Company of Others: An Introduction to Communication*, Dan Rothwell has identified 5 key elements for active listening.

1. *Pay attention*
   - Give the speaker your undivided attention and acknowledge the message
   - Recognize that non-verbal communication also "speaks" loudly.
   - Look at the speaker directly.
   - Put aside distracting thoughts. Don't mentally prepare a rebuttal.
   - Avoid being distracted by environmental factors.
   - "*Listen*" to the speaker's body language.
   - Refrain from side conversations when listening in a group setting.

2. *Show that you are listening*
   - Use your own body language and gestures to convey your attention.
   - Nod occasionally.
   - Smile and use other facial expressions.
   - Note your posture and make sure it is open and inviting.
   - Encourage the speaker to continue with small verbal comments like yes, and uh huh.

3. ***Provide feedback***
    - Our personal filters, assumptions, judgments, and beliefs can distort what we hear. As a listener, your role is to understand what is being said. This may require you to reflect what is being said and ask questions.
    - Reflect what has been said by paraphrasing. *"What I'm hearing is...", and "Sounds like you are saying..."*
    - Ask questions to clarify certain points. *"What do you mean when you say..." "Is this what you mean? "*
    - Summarize the speaker's comments periodically.

4. ***Defer judgment***
    - Interrupting is a waste of time. It frustrates the speaker and limits full understanding of the message.
    - Allow the speaker to finish.
    - Don't interrupt with counter arguments.

5. ***Respond appropriately***
    - Active listening is a model for respect and understanding. You are gaining information and perspective. You add nothing by attacking the speaker or otherwise putting them down.
    - Be candid, open, and honest in your response.
    - Assert your opinions respectfully.
    - Treat the other person as you would want to be treated.

For older students, middle-high school age, I recommend putting these key elements on a chart, explaining the importance of them, in a few words, and, not only modeling them, but refer to them as often as possible throughout the school year.

Daily Assignment #98: Student's Body Language

Body language, as we all know is, **not** a true indicator of students' attention. Body language can be very deceptive. While some body language signs are obvious, it's hard for a teacher not to assume the worst. We've all had students who appear very engaged and aren't. And then we have those that don't look like they are engaged at all, or even know where they are, and actually are engaged.

During instruction there will be some students nodding their heads, thumbing through the text, or diligently taking notes. Are they the ones paying attention? I know students who have said they do these behaviors so that the teacher will think they are following the lesson.

And then, how about the student who the minute you ask a question their head goes down and they look busy, as if they are looking through their notes for the answer? They know that if they make eye contact with the teacher, or don't look busy, they may be called on. I confess I've done this move. They are totally trying not to be noticed.

Then there are the students whose eyes become glassed over, or their bodies are completely turned around, or they are tapping their fingers, or playing with something or shifting around in their seat. They appear to be doing everything but paying attention.

A student with a bowed head may be listening in rapt concentration, whereas from the front of the room, they appear to be taking a nap.

I have experienced all these scenarios. What I've learned, as a result, is not to be so quick to assume the worst.

One of the goals of all teachers is to gain and maintain our students' attention throughout our instruction. The reality is that students will drift off and come back once, if not several times, during the instruction, especially if you're speaking longer than thirty minutes. As a matter of fact, for maximum impact teachers should try not to instruct for more than 10-12 minutes at a time, as I mentioned in Daily Assignment # 95: Teacher Talk.

CHAPTER 9: END OF THE YEAR

Daily Assignment #99: Retention-- Making That Tough Decision

By now, you have probably identified a student who is not yet ready to face the challenges of the next grade level. This is a difficult decision, and one not to be taken lightly. I have yet to meet a teacher who hasn't agonized over broaching this subject with parents. As difficult as it is, parents should be given a heads up long before May. However, if you haven't yet given one, all is not lost. Still discuss retention with parents at this point. I have found most parents are not surprised when the idea of retention is brought up. They usually have had questions and doubts about promotion also. Whatever the situation parents must be involved in this decision, as well as the administrator.

So, when do you retain a student? In my opinion, you just don't retain a child because his/her academics are not on grade level. Instead, look at the whole child. A friend, and former principal, recommended that I use Light's Retention Scale when I was struggling over retaining a student. I gave a copy to the student's parents to fill out, and I completed one as well. It was very interesting. When we did the scoring of both forms, the scores actually came out the same. The scores indicated that the student would be a "Good Retention Candidate".

Here are the 19 categories that are covered:

1. Knowledge of English Language
2. Physical Size of the Student
3. Student's Age
4. Sex of Student
5. Siblings
6. Parents' School Participation
7. Transiency

8. School Attendance
9. Present Level of Academic Achievement
10. Student's Attitude About Possible Retention
11. Present Grade Placement
12. Previous Grade retention
13. Immature Behavior
14. Emotional Problems
15. History of Delinquency
16. Experiential Background
17. Motivation to Complete School Task
18. History of Learning Disabilities
19. Estimate of Intelligence

Each response has a numeric value.

For example:
Knowledge of English Language:
- Student has good communication skills using the English language..0
- Student has limited use of the English language but is acquiring new skills quickly...................2
- Student has little or no knowledge of the English language and is not acquiring new skills............5

At the end of the 19 categories, total the numbers and compare to the Interpretation Guidelines Table.
Example: A total score of 0-9: Excellent retention candidate.

This is the link to Light's Retention Scale:
www.boarddocs.com/wcps/.../Light's%20Retention%20Scale.pdf

This tool should not be used as the only method of determining a student's retention. It is another aid to help in that decision.

Once everyone has agreed that retention would be the best plan for a student, someone has to tell the student. Some parents prefer to do it themselves.

Other parents prefer that the teacher tells the student, and then the parent does follow-up conversations at home. Some parents and teachers jointly tell the student.

In most cases, when I retained a student, the parents and I told the student jointly. We would meet with the student at the very end of the year, but before move-up day.

The conversation would begin with a question for the student, such as "How do you feel the school year went for you?" With follow-up questions: "What was your favorite subject?" "What did you like best?" "What did you find challenging?" "Was there something you would like to have more time to learn or something you would like to improve on?" "What do you feel was the hardest/most challenging subject?"

I would then explain that... "Some students just need a little more time to learn math or reading, or whatever. It is like that for everything we do. There are some things I can do really well and there are some things I need more time to learn. That is true for everyone."

Give examples of things that the student does well, and then what he/she needs to work on. Do not give a laundry list of what the student needs to improve on. That can be overwhelming.

Mention only a few areas that need improvement. Have the parents share areas where they have had to spend a lot of time learning something - hopefully a school-related topic.

Tell the student how fortunate he/she is to have adults who want to make sure their learning is right where it should be before they go to the next grade level. "So, we, your parents and I, have decided we are going to give you that time to make your learning the best it can be at this grade level. You are going to spend another year in grade_____, to make sure you are totally ready for grade _____."

Let that settle in for a few seconds. Then clarify any questions the student might have. Most importantly, be as reassuring as possible. Make sure the student understands that they have done nothing wrong. This is all about learning and being well prepared for the next level.

If possible, let the student know who the teacher will be for the new school year. Arrange for the student to visit the new class. Check to see if the student has any friends going into that class as well. Suggest to the parents to arrange for play dates during the summer to help build relationships within the new class.

Now, having said all that, please know that this strategy is not researched-based. It is experienced-based. It is what worked best for me, my families, and my students. I hope it will help you with your conversation with a student you may be retaining.

Daily Assignment #101: Closure for the End of the Year, Portfolio Presentations

An activity I did with students the last week of school was Portfolio Presentations. I would meet with each student 2-3 weeks before the end of school and go through their work--math, writing, projects, drawings, journals, assessments.

Students would select a piece of work from the beginning of the year and one from the same content area from the end of the year. We would conference on the significance of the selected work, e.g. why it was chosen, what it represents for the student, what is the difference between the 2 pieces of work, what did the student learn that makes the difference, can they demonstrate the learning. The students would write their responses, which were used for their oral presentation.

Examples:

Math: The student selects a worksheet from September that demonstrates his capacity to do simple equations. The second worksheet-one from May-represents the student's capacity to solve 3-digit subtraction equations with regrouping. For the presentation the student would read their responses to the questions and then demonstrate how to solve a 3-digit subtraction equation with regrouping.

Reading: The student selects a book they read in September and then a book they are currently reading. They respond to the questions. For the presentation the student would read the responses, and then read a passage from the first book and one from the latest book.

Writing: The student would select a piece from the beginning of the year and a current piece. For the presentation the student would read their responses then share their work. We did this by copying the writing onto a transparency, or by using an Elmo, or copying onto a computer and showing on a Smart board.

Art: The student selects a piece of art from the beginning of the year, perhaps a drawing, and a piece from the end of the year. For the presentation the student reads their responses, shares the artwork, and demonstrates/describes a technique that they have learned.

Music: The student selects a piece of music they learned at the beginning of the year and one they currently play or sing. For the presentation they read their responses, play or sing the 1st piece, then the 2nd. To take this to the next level, students could write their own piece of music to play or sing.

The presentations were done as part of a class breakfast. Parents, families, colleagues, administrators and anyone else who wanted to came to this event. It was very powerful to hear and see the students share their learning. The students took this event very seriously and really put in the effort into the presentations.

Daily Assignment #102: Closure for the End of the Year: Goodbye Book

Another activity for the end of the year is a "Goodbye Book". This provides a brief summary of the school year for the students.
The teacher puts the name of the class and the year on the front cover.
The students complete the cover by decorating it with drawings of things that happened throughout the year.

On the inside have 8-10 pages with ideas for drawings or words.
For example:
Draw a picture of your teachers.
Draw a picture of a friend.
Something you learned.
Favorite field trip.
Something that made you laugh.
Favorite activity.
Favorite book.
Something I shared.
Something I'm good at.
Favorite project.
Favorite unit of study.
Autograph pages/ a gift from a friend. (The gift from the friend would be kind words.)
A gift from your teacher. (Again, this would be kind words.)

Match the ideas to your class and your students. I'm sure you have a lot more ideas.

On a side note, I spoke with a student today who I had 15 years ago. She said she still has her book! So, these are definitely keepers.

Daily Assignment #103: Closure for the End of the Year, Letters to "New Students"

This strategy is for the very beginning of community building for the new school year and a way for current students to "pass the wand" to the new students.

Each current student writes a letter to an incoming student for the next school year. The letter should include a sentence welcoming the new student to the class, one or two sentences about projects and activities that were done this year, and perhaps a sentence on their favorite thing in the classroom.

Students should use the formal letter-writing format. Each letter should begin with "Dear...." and end with "Your Friend" or "Sincerely Yours".

Example:

Dear_____,

    Welcome to room 103.

    This is such an exciting class to be in. This year we studied islands and got to make volcanoes. We also studied Social Justice. We did a play based on the Montgomery Boycott. You probably don't know what that is yet, but you will.

    My favorite thing in the classroom is the art area. We get to use clay, paints, markers, and other neat stuff.

    I hope you have as much fun as me in room 103.

Your friend,
Benjamin

You may not have a class list for next September and therefore you cannot identify to whom each letter is to be addressed. So, just have the students write "Dear" and leave a blank which you will fill in later.

Two weeks before school begins, send one of these letters and a welcoming letter from you to each of your new students. (refer to Daily Assignment #1) This, of course, will require you to find a safe place for the letters over the summer and to remember where you put them.

CHAPTER 10: FINAL THOUGHTS

Daily Assignment #104: Qualities of Highly Effective Teachers

I would like to end this book with an inspirational/motivational piece.

"7 Qualities of Highly Effective Teachers," by Linc. Fisch.

1. *Highly effective teachers care.* They care about their students, their work, and themselves. They treat others with dignity; they respect others' integrity. They give high priority to benefiting others. They affirm others' strengths and beings; it's a kind of love.

2. *Highly effective teachers share.* They share their knowledge, insights, and viewpoints with others. Their willingness to share is a way of life for them. They don't withhold information for personal gain.

3. *Highly effective teachers learn.* They continually seek truth and meaning. They seek to discover new ideas and insights. They reflect on their experiences and incorporate the learning into their lives. They are willing to upgrade their skills. They continue growing and developing throughout their lives.

4. *Highly effective teachers create.* They are willing to try the new and untested, to take risks for worthy educational outcomes. Anything worth doing is worth failing at. They are not discouraged by an occasional failure; they re-frame the error as an opportunity to do better as a result of the experience.

5. *Highly effective teachers believe.* They have faith in students. They trust students and are willing to grant them freedom and responsibility. They hold high expectations for their students, as well as for themselves.

6. *Highly effective teachers dream.* They have a vision of success. They are driven by an image of excellence, the best that their innate abilities

allow. They always seek to improve, never being content with just "getting by" in teaching or in any other endeavor.

7. *Highly effective teachers enjoy.* Teaching is not just employment to them; it is their Work. They throw themselves into it with vigor. They gain major satisfaction and joy from it. And that joy often infects their students.

I hope this inspires you and reaffirms all the hard work that you do.

Daily Assignment #105: Legacy

A dear friend, and colleague, Jane, asked me what I wanted my legacy to teaching to be when I retired. I believe it is the hope of all teachers that something taught, or done through the years, impacts a student or colleague in away that the spirit of the lesson/experience carries on years after we have left the profession. However, for me, I couldn't figure out what that was.

After watching a video by Sir Ken Robinson, I realized what I would like to be my legacy. I want people to say that, "Linda taught the total child." When I reflect on my 34 years of teaching, I recognize that I not only taught the core content areas, but I also included ceramics, orienteering, recorders, ballroom dancing, dramatizations, plays, knitting, singing, art, and things I can't even remember. Please know, I did not do this all alone. Parents and volunteers supported my classroom on a regular basis. An amazing parent- Barb Bryant, volunteered to teach orienteering for many years. There was another parent, Lucia Mudd, who taught ceramics, and a group of mothers who came in once a week, to teach knitting - just to mention a few. So, you see, it does take a village.

I hope by watching this video you will become, if not already, more cognizant of how you integrate music, art, physical movement, or whatever else you can do to tap into a child's interest, strengths, and most importantly, the creative part of their brain.

This video is 19 minutes long. It is well worth your time. It is humorous, while making an important point. So, please take the time to watch: http://www.youtube.com/embed/iG9CE55wbtY

Acknowledgements

I would like to thank my family for their support, especially my son Tim. Tim suggested that I start a blog -which has now turned into this book- to share my 35 years of experience as a teacher.

Thank you to my husband who has always supported and cheered me on.

Thank you to my son Michael who helped with the design of the cover and drawings and to my son Jonathan, who gave me feedback on each entry from afar.

Thank you to Brianna Goldberg for her endless support for over 15 years, not only as a former student, volunteer, and friend and now for letting me come into her own classroom and continue my connection with teaching.

Thank you to Julia Bishop, Jane Donohue, Bill Chipman, Karen Bondi, Beth Noe, Len Solo, and Joe Petner for their support and encouragement.

A huge thank you to Bill Bramham for patiently editing this book.

To everyone else who gave me feedback, suggestions, and support while writing this book, and you know who you are, I thank you.

And a special thank you to all the children that were my guinea pigs as I experimented with all the strategies that are contained in this book. Each one of you made me the teacher I have become.

Bibliography

Bloom, Benjamin S., (Ed.), *Taxonomy of Education Objectives: Handbook I: Cognitive Domain*, N.Y., David McKay Company, Inc. 1956.

Burns, Deborah, "Taxonomy of Type II Process Skills," 1994, University of Connecticut:
http://www.gifted.uconn.edu/sem/typeiips.html?

Caram, Chris; Davis, Patsy B.,"Inviting Student Engagement with Questioning". Kappa Delta Pi Record, Vol. 42, 2005.

Cooper, Harris M., *The Battle Over Homework: Common Ground for Administrators, Teachers and Parents*, Corwin Press, 2007

Fisch, Linc., The Chalk Dust Collection: Thoughts and Reflections on Teaching in Colleges & Universities, New Forums Press, Inc., 1996.

Gardner, H., *Multiple Intelligences: The Theory in Practice*, New York: Basic Books, 1999.

Gordon, Thomas, *P.E.T.: Parent Effectiveness Training,* Three River Press, N.Y., 1970.

Hunter, Madeline, *Enhancing Teaching*, Prentice Hall, 1993.

Kagan, Spencer, Kagan Cooperative Learning, Kagan Publishing, 2008.

Kounin, Jacob, *Discipline and Group Management in Classrooms,* Huntington, N.Y., R. E. Krieger, 1977.

Lights Retention Scale:
www.boarddocs.com/wcps/.../Light's%20Retention%20Scale.pdf
Marzano, Robert; Pickering, D., Pollock,J., *Classroom Instruction That Works: Research-Based Strategies for Increasing Student Achievement*, ASCD, 2001.

McNaughty, David; Vostel, Brooks, "Using Active Listening to Improve Collaboration with Parents: The LAFF Don't CRY Strategy," Sage Publications and Hammill Institute on Disabilities, 2008.

McTighe, Jay; O'Connor,Ken, "Seven Practices for Effective Learning," Educational Leadership, November 2005, Volume 63.

Pauk, Walter, *How to Study in College 7/e*, Houghton Mifflin, 2001

Rhem, James, "Pygmalion In The Classroom," NTFL, February1999, Vol. 8.

Robinson, Sir Ken: http://www.youtube.com/embed/iG9CE55wbtY

Rosenthal, Robert; Jacobson, Lenore, *Pygmalion in the Classroom: Teacher Expectation and Pupils' Intellectual Development*, Holt, Rinehart and Winston, 1968.

Rothwell, Dan, *In Company of Others: An Introduction to Communication*, McGraw-Hill, 1999

Saphier, Jon; Haley, Mary Ann, Activators: Activity Structures to Engage Students' Thinking Before Instruction, Research for Better Teaching, 1994.

Saphier, Jon; Haley-Speca, Mary Ann; Gower, Robert, *The Skillful Teacher: Building Your Teaching Skills*, Research for Better Teaching, 2008.

Stanford Literacy Improvement Project: http://www.stanford.edu/group/SLIP/TIPS/Teaching.html.

Taba, Hilda, *Curriculum Development: Theory and Practice* , Harcourt, Brace & World, 1962.

Teacher Vision: http://www.teachervision.fen.com/skill-builder/problem-solving/48546.html?page=1.

Wiggins, Grant, "Feedback: How Learning Occurs," 2010.

17662179R10097

Made in the USA
Lexington, KY
06 October 2012